Data-Driven Decision Making

A Handbook *for* School Leaders

CHRIS O'NEAL

International Society for Technology in Education
EUGENE, OREGON • WASHINGTON, DC

Data-Driven Decision Making
A Handbook for School Leaders

Chris O'Neal

© 2012 International Society for Technology in Education

World rights reserved. No part of this book may be reproduced or transmitted in any form or by any means—electronic, mechanical, photocopying, recording, or by any information storage or retrieval system—without prior written permission from the publisher. Contact Permissions Editor: www.iste.org/learn/publications/permissions-and-reprints.aspx; permissions@iste.org; fax: 1.541.302.3780.

Director of Book Publishing: *Courtney Burkholder*
Acquisitions Editor: *Jeff V. Bolkan*
Production Editors: *Lynda Gansel, Tina Wells*
Production Coordinator: *Rachel Williams*
Graphic Designer: *Signe Landin*
Copy Editor: *Kristin Landon*
Proofreader: *Ann Skaugset*
Cover Design, Book Design, and Production: *Kathy Sturtevant*

Library of Congress Cataloging-in-Publication Data

O'Neal, Chris.
Data-driven decision making : a handbook for school leaders / Chris O'Neal. — 1st ed.
   p. cm.
 ISBN 978-1-56484-308-1 (pbk.)
 1. School management and organization—Decision making—Data processing. I. Title.
LB2806.17.O64 2012
371.2—dc23

                                                                       2011039119

First Edition
ISBN: 978-1-56484-308-1
Printed in the United States of America

Cover art: © istockphoto.com/CTRdesign; *Cover photo:* © istockphoto.com/Joshua Hodge Photography *Inside photos:* pg. 1: © istockphoto.com/Tamara Murray; pg. 7: © istockphoto.com/Rudyanto Wijaya; pg. 15: © istockphoto.com/Stígur Karlsson; pg. 41: © istockphoto.com/ewg3D; pg. 59: © istockphoto.com/loops7; pg. 73: © istockphoto.com/Jacob Wackerhausen; pg. 83: © istockphoto.com/Nicole Waring

About ISTE

The International Society for Technology in Education (ISTE) is the trusted source for professional development, knowledge generation, advocacy, and leadership for innovation. ISTE is the premier membership association for educators and education leaders engaged in improving teaching and learning by advancing the effective use of technology in PK–12 and teacher education.

Home of the National Educational Technology Standards (NETS) and ISTE's annual conference and exposition (formerly known as NECC), ISTE represents more than 100,000 professionals worldwide. We support our members with information, networking opportunities, and guidance as they face the challenge of transforming education. To find out more about these and other ISTE initiatives, visit our website at www.iste.org.

As part of our mission, ISTE Book Publishing works with experienced educators to develop and produce practical resources for classroom teachers, teacher educators, and technology leaders. Every manuscript we select for publication is carefully peer-reviewed and professionally edited. We value your feedback on this book and other ISTE products. Email us at books@iste.org.

International Society for Technology in Education

Washington, DC, Office:
    1710 Rhode Island Ave. NW, Suite 900, Washington, DC 20036-3132

Eugene, Oregon, Office:
    180 West 8th Ave., Suite 300, Eugene, OR 97401-2916

Order Desk: 1.800.336.5191
Order Fax: 1.541.302.3778
Customer Service: orders@iste.org
Book Publishing: books@iste.org
Book Sales and Marketing: booksmarketing@iste.org
Web: www.iste.org

About the Author

Chris O'Neal is a former elementary and middle school teacher. During his time in the classroom, he received numerous teacher of the year honors. After leaving the classroom, Chris went on to work in the curriculum and instruction office for the school district. There he worked with teachers in high-risk schools to enhance classroom practice through the use of new teaching strategies and tools. He also developed content to support high-risk classrooms and provided professional development to teachers and administrators. He later worked at the State Department of Education in Louisiana, focusing on grant management, policy and planning issues, district support, and eventually becoming the director of educational technology for the State of Louisiana. His work with the governor's office and the legislature earned him status as an honorary state senator. He has also been featured as a "Shaper of Our Future" in *Converge* magazine, and received the "Making IT Happen" award for leaders in the field of education. He is a featured speaker each year at the International Society for Technology in Education (ISTE) annual conference and has served as a faculty associate for the George Lucas Educational Foundation.

O'Neal provides leadership professional development, content development, and consulting for ISTE; conducts educational leadership institutes, workshops, and evaluations for several districts around the world, and has served as a leadership facilitator for SETDA (the U.S. State Educational Technology Directors Association). He also leads numerous large scale projects including 1-to-1 laptop initiatives, and iPod and iPad pilots.

Contents

Introduction

IF YOU ask educators to describe their school's or district's data-driven decision making efforts, many will simply describe their process for analyzing standardized test scores. True data-driven decision making, however, is about more than just test scores. It's about exploring the overall health and well-being of a district or school. It's about asking all the players in the school community to provide feedback on an ongoing basis. We expect doctors to keep immaculate records of our health and to suggest care and treatment based on individualized data and ongoing research. Our schools should operate with similar aspirations. A data-driven school or district keeps data at the forefront of professional development planning, budgeting, curriculum development, classroom instruction, and administrative leadership. Throughout this book, we'll take a look at this broader view of data to help guide us to a more authentically connected educational community. We'll examine strategies to guide our efforts as school leaders; solidify our school communities around common, data-informed conversations; and ultimately improve the academic experiences of our students.

This book is meant to be a practical handbook that helps leaders take action based on existing theory, and helps districts implement strategies in a practical way in order to enrich and sustain school improvement efforts.

For the purposes of this book, I will first define *data-driven decision making* (3D) as the ongoing cycle of making choices and taking action based on multiple sources of data and frequent, thoughtful conversations with the larger school community. Additionally, I consider the process of data-driven decision making to be a mindset that is ingrained into the culture of a school or other organization. I will use the term *leader* to informally designate someone within a school or district who takes the initiative to move school improvement forward. That may be a principal at an individual school who has decided to take this charge and lead the way. It might also be a technology coordinator within a building who wants to push this effort along by assembling others to help. It could refer to a team of leaders at a central office who have been assigned the task of data-driven decision making or school improvement and must achieve the effort across multiple schools. In any of these situations, the materials in this book can easily be adapted to suit the role of the leader, no matter what his or her official title may be.

> Data-driven decision making (3D): the ongoing cycle of making choices based on multiple sources of data and frequent, thoughtful conversations

Considerations of data often focus on end-of-year summative test scores, chapter tests, and six-week report cards. These indicators give us a big, but shallow, picture of what we need to know about the performance of our students. Students who make good grades and score well enough on standardized tests might be deemed successful. These indicators may broadly depict how a student's performance conforms to our content standards—but unless we ask deeper questions and examine more formative assessments along the way, we can't be certain we're looking at an accurate portrayal of what the student is accomplishing. In addition, without continuous rich conversations about what's going on around us, any subpar performance issues aren't likely to change.

Authentic data-driven decision making is an entire framework in which teachers, principals, students, parents, central-office staff, community members, and others look closely at performance issues, map out strategic plans to address these issues, and work together as a cohesive team to make changes where needed. A true indication of a school or district's success involves a multitude of indicators beyond the ones we traditionally examine. Student attitudes toward the school community, parental voices, board directives, and public expectations all provide valuable contributions to the bigger picture of a data-informed district or school.

In recent years, there has been a strong push for schools and districts to pay even more attention to test scores and performance gains. The debate continues about the benefits and drawbacks of increased attention to standardized test scores as a public school and district scoring mechanism. However, few would dispute that this increased focus has at least advanced conversations regarding equity of access, traditionally underperforming populations, and growth for all students.

I suggest that it has also done something else. It has forced each of us to be more open about analyzing not only the performance of our students but the performance of our leadership at all levels: teachers, principals, curriculum directors, school board members, and so on. It has also given us a setting in which we may become more accustomed to putting our strengths and weaknesses out on the table for everyone to see. Traditionally, the atmosphere in education has been less than accommodating toward open discussions of test score performance with a large audience. Now, we have no choice. Our test scores are displayed, published, printed, compared, and analyzed for the world to see. Our reactions to that must be forthright and productive. We must be proactive in promoting the good things going on in our districts while admitting any mistakes we may have made. We must be open to input from a variety of sources. We must actively seek and accept help from all levels. Time is of the essence: our students and the quality of education in which they are immersed must both advance.

Educators at all levels must be savvy users of data. Leaders must be able to understand and examine various forms of data, assess and track progress, identify patterns of performance, and weave this information throughout every aspect of their jobs. By modeling a constant and thoughtful use of data, leaders set the tone for a system ready to move forward as a unified front. We must ensure that every person in the district recognizes that they have a genuine role in the success of the educational environment and that their role contributes to, and is driven by, data. The superintendent- and cabinet-level leadership must model this ideal by making sure that each decision considers data in a legitimate way. Leadership staff must be solid in their decision-making processes and in sharing how and why decisions are made. Doing so can help build trust and buy-in from teachers and others throughout the district.

Book Structure

In this book, we'll be looking at data issues in the form of a workbook. The activities in this book are designed to be as efficient as possible in building and engaging educational teams in thoughtful data-related endeavors. A cycle like the one shown in Figure I.1 can help keep improvement efforts on track, and keep the focus on practicality and time well spent.

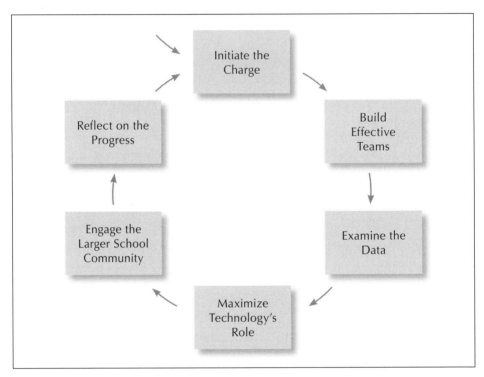

Figure I.1. A practical cycle for leading a data-driven decision making effort.

Some districts and schools may feel that they are ready to forge ahead and get into school data analysis at a deep level rather quickly, or even skip ahead to working with the larger school or district audience. In any case, it is important that each school spend ample time on setting the stage, encouraging the data-informed mindset, and working to continuously cultivate and reenergize a data-informed way of thinking. In this book, I focus on the teamwork and team-building aspects of data-driven decision making and strategies to synchronize the efforts of an educational team.

Numerous books and publications exist that will help you read and analyze test scores and understand the mechanics of data warehouse management software and hardware. A gap seems to exist, however, for the nontechnical and nonnumber-crunching view of data-driven decision making. This workbook will supplement the great work that's out there by presenting concepts in a language that all the players can understand and in a format that everyone can use right away.

Throughout the rest of this book, examples and exercises are provided for both a school-level effort and a district-level effort. Suggestions, tables, and templates are developed for both of these perspectives, and you should adapt them based on the makeup of your organization. Worksheets are provided at the end of the chapter in which they are mentioned.

For each of these resources, you are urged to examine the content or issue from both the school *and* district perspective, because every district is structured differently. Some school-based suggestions might work perfectly for a small district, for example. Some school improvement teams are made up of both central-office and school-based staff, so looking at ideas from both levels might provide the clearest focus.

CHAPTER 1

Initiating the Charge

MOST EDUCATORS want to make the most informed decisions possible. That's common sense. There isn't enough time or money in education to go on hunches, shoot from the hip, or stick with the status quo if we find things aren't working as we'd like. Each of us needs to reflect on what decisions we make and what data we consider when making those decisions. That isn't to suggest that we form a task force every time we want to address a small issue. It does mean, however, that we should reflect on the actions we take and consider analyzing those actions to see how they affect student learning or some other educational goal. It also means once we do discover some potential issues with performance, we discuss them and address them in an open, timely, professional, and direct manner.

Data-driven mentality is really a culture of thought—not something we do as part of an isolated workshop or as an added layer on top of an already busy schedule. In addition to that, it is important that the term *data* come to encompass an idea much bigger than test scores. As educational leaders, we need to promote buy-in to this mindset in a genuine way and ensure that all the key players understand how data affects their jobs.

Establish the Mindset

Efficiency in time, budgets, and efforts is a vital piece of a well-run system and a high-performing school. Being able to take a step back and make thoughtful observations across the district will increase the overall health of the system and the effectiveness of its players. But these efforts do not always come naturally in the hurry of the school day or year. Taking charge of this effort, helping others see their roles, and keeping the effort moving forward can become habit. Continuing to ask questions, examining information, and justifing decisions through data-informed conversations can help enrich the quality of education at all levels within a school or district. Being a leader in this effort means we continuously ask ourselves, "Why are we headed in this direction? Why this program at this time? Who is concretely addressing this specific performance issue we've uncovered?" It is up to each of us to be forthright in advancing this agenda and modeling this mindset of continuous use of information.

Establishing a default protocol for all staff meetings, professional development initiatives, grants, and other efforts, in which *everyone* gets into the habit of asking questions about data and makes a pointed effort to establish strong bonds across departments, helps guarantee a more tightly knit district, stronger by number and mission.

Think of changing school and district direction as turning a huge ship around in a river. It can be done, but it takes planning and effort. It takes people on the sidelines looking at the task from various angles. It takes people on board, with clear lines of communication, all working in unison toward the same direction and the same vision. Most of all, it takes teamwork and commitment.

Each of the following roles clearly has a part in improving student achievement even if there is no direct contact with students in the schools. Consider the connections between data and each of the following roles.

CLASSROOM TEACHERS

Teachers learn early on to rely on test results as *one* component to help inform the whole picture of the child. But recognizing individual traits, personal strengths and challenges, interests, and so on helps them determine how to reach individual students. Teachers need access to targeted resources, shared leadership, cooperative guidance from their peers, and clear direction from the organization as a whole to use data effectively, and gain traction toward improving instructional efforts. Teachers also need to be part of frequent, focused conversations in which they are able to dig down into performance data, identify the most concrete problems or concerns to be addressed, and share strategies for taking action on these. Teachers should be able to count on data-informed professional development assistance that matches the needs of their school and classroom.

PRINCIPALS

A principal's job is massive—no one would argue with that. Principals are in charge of student learning, teacher professional development, scheduling, busing, discipline, parental issues, physical plant issues, budgets, and more. Data that can show connections among these issues is crucial to making the most informed decisions. Principals must have access to data warehouses that can tie all these issues together. Further, they must have the knowledge to examine each of these issues with various lenses. Ensuring that principals have access to, and can understand, the interconnectedness among these layers is truly a foundation for successful leadership efforts.

SUPERINTENDENTS, DEPUTY SUPERINTENDENTS, AND ASSISTANT SUPERINTENDENTS

Clearly, data-informed modeling by top-level leadership staff is essential to becoming a truly data-driven district. The values, messages, and attitudes of top-level staff have dramatic influence on the seriousness with which school staff buys into the data-driven model. Teachers must feel assured that central-office leadership staff are engaged in frequent conversations with each other in which they assess their own performance including hiring processes, internal structures of support, purchasing decisions, professional development assistance, and so on. In short, top-level leadership staff must make sure that from one end of the district to the other, decisions are made based on valid information and need.

DATA OR TESTING COORDINATORS

A testing coordinator is generally well versed in understanding all the various student tests, reports, and accountability components. In addition, these leaders are probably the ones who have direct communications with board members and state agencies regarding testing timelines, requirements, and reporting issues. Further, they are in touch with testing vendors who provide support with understanding terminology, published report formats, reading test results, and so forth. Therefore, a data or testing coordinator plays a central role in the overall picture of data-driven decision making. Misinterpretation of data and misreading of reports can have damaging effects on students. A testing coordinator can lead the data charge by ensuring that there is common and correct understanding of data and testing-related terms, and that those who are involved in analyzing data are interpreting reports and results correctly. Ensuring that data-related terms are used appropriately and uniformly can help establish a clear and solid understanding of school improvement as it relates to data. Decisions along the way should always include input from a data or testing coordinator, and this person should be active and visible throughout all aspects of any improvement efforts.

BOARD MEMBERS

Board members are very important in helping shape and refine policy issues that support data-driven decision making. They should also be accurately informed when talking to community members about district and school growth issues, as they relate to data. By taking part in informational data conversations, they can be in a better position to counteract negative impressions of school performance or correct misinformed public perceptions. A board member is a direct connection from the classroom to the public at large. This line of communication must be well informed regarding student performance issues and efforts by the district to speak to these issues. In addition, school board members should help ensure district and school direction, by questioning connections between data and existing and upcoming initiatives.

PROFESSIONAL DEVELOPMENT COORDINATORS

In a data-driven system, *all* staff development must use performance data as a backdrop against which professional development offerings are built. Workshops that are singular in nature, or simply "how-to" by design, might not be as effective as those built on specific classroom needs. For example, a workshop on "The Wonderful World of Wikis" that is developed simply to show a new tool might better serve teachers if it were angled more toward a student performance issue. A professional development coordinator might still create a wiki workshop, but it might, for example, be geared toward a focused subset of language arts teachers who have identified students with collaborative writing needs.

In addition, teachers might be required to bring the previous year's summative assessment class scores with them to a data overview workshop, or perhaps a few months' worth of formative assessment samples to a series of science workshops, for example. Ongoing professional development, in which teachers continuously reflect on the applicability of the topic at hand and its connection to their specific classroom performance issues, helps to ensure a more focused and efficient return on time invested. Ensuring that staff development plans from all departments are in sync with relevant data issues improves the efficiency and outcome of these efforts across the board. A professional development coordinator can serve as the "hub" for training and workshops, ensuring that overlap is avoided and that time spent in professional development is focused on identified growth needs.

TECHNOLOGY COORDINATORS

Both types of technology coordinators—the instructional and the technical—have important roles in data-driven districts. Consider the impact a well-run, efficient, and teacher-friendly information systems interface can have on the use of data. Many teachers are fearful of looking at and mining for performance data, but a technical coordinator can ensure that data access is easy and smooth, removing obstacles for those who are new to data analysis. Instructional technology personnel should be well versed in the overall performance data of the students and teachers they work with, to make sure the technology efforts are directly connected to identified data needs. Gone are the days of teaching the masses how to use "cool" technology tools just for the sake of using them, or seeking out the latest gadgets just because they're available. Technology training should have clear curricular goals in mind, be connected to data and improvement efforts, and help advance instructional efforts to take advantage of new ways of teaching and learning.

SPECIAL EDUCATION COORDINATORS

It is important for all instructional staff to be aware of data and performance issues, even with students they may not ever teach. Making certain that traditional classroom teachers, administrators, department heads, and other employees are well versed in the unique issues that are a part of special education can help ensure a smooth data cycle and ultimately lead to big improvement gains for both special education and traditional students. Many times the techniques that special education teachers use with their students can have direct applicability in the regular classroom. Therefore, it is important that data conversations include input from special education, and that leaders set out to remove any barriers between traditional and special education classrooms and initiatives.

FEDERAL PROGRAM COORDINATORS

Using performance data as a framework for budgeting and for assignment of aides and other personnel ensures the biggest impact of federal- and state-level funding. In addition, title-funded schools traditionally serve a population who may not come to school with the advantages of students who don't qualify for federal funding. Thus, it's important to make sure that efforts in these schools can be clearly tied to performance issues. School-based personnel who are funded from federal and state budgets must clearly understand their roles and the data issues in the schools and classrooms to which they are assigned, to ensure that they, too, are directing their efforts accordingly. Federal program personnel can typically offer a broad view of improvement efforts based on the sheer number of schools they serve. That expertise is crucial to any school improvement team.

AUXILIARY SERVICES

Other education personnel—from transportation supervisor to child nutrition director to public relations officer—should also be a part of ongoing data discussions. Having noninstructional staff be a part of data conversations will help solidify the data improvement team and its efforts. For example, engage transportation staff in discussions about maximizing learning time: Are our bus schedules set up for maximum time on academics? In light of specific student performance trends, might we be able to get students at low-performing schools into their classrooms a few minutes earlier? Shall we open up a media lab for some before-school or after-school remediation? Making certain that every office in the district is involved in instructional conversations can only help the wheel spin more efficiently.

Reflect on Big-Picture Questions Early On

Data analysis isn't only about stanines, scaled scores, and the like, or even about meeting accountability requirements. It's about monitoring the overall well-being of a learning system. The cycle involves looking at the data, taking action on what's discovered, checking in frequently to monitor the progress, and making changes when the progress isn't what is desired. Use Worksheet 1 to take a broad look at your school or district.

A Broad Look at Your School or District

Before exploring the resources and strategies in this book, think "big picture" and consider the following questions:

- Generally speaking, what is it about our district's or school's performance that works well?

- Are there common concerns that are heard across the school? Across the district?

- Where do we stand in regard to accountability requirements? Where are we headed?

- Are there incorrect assumptions—internally or externally—about our district or school performance?

- What do I already know about student performance data in my school or district? What do other staff members within the district or building know?

- Am I comfortable reading student performance data in its various formats?

- Do we have data warehouse or management tools that let me customize the way I view or interact with data?

- What school improvement efforts are in place, and where does data fit into those efforts? How effectively does it fit? Do all team players use this data?

- If a school improvement plan already exists, is it truly in sync with what our data tells us? How do we know? If the plan is not in sync, what is the process for updating it?

- What procedures are in place to help us take action and carry forth our school improvement plan?

- How will we measure the changes we'd like to see?

- Do we communicate regularly and effectively with the broader educational audience?

- Is our team in unison in its efforts?

- How can I be a positive force in solidifying our district or school team structure?

2

Building an Effective 3D Team and Culture

ONE OF the most critical, yet often overlooked, components in a highly effective, data-informed educational entity is the synchronicity of all its players. In this chapter, we'll explore some basic, practical ideas for creating effective data-driven decision making (3D) teams. Some of the principles we'll discuss are common across typical school improvement teams and professional learning communities.

This chapter will focus primarily on the work of the team as it relates to:

- facilitating more well-informed conversations;

- building a healthier team environment;

- helping to enlighten decisions with a more thoughtful look at data;

- encouraging ongoing and productive communications with the broader educational community;

- leading change efforts.

Creating a core 3D group to help lead the data-driven decision making charge is important because (1) one person can't lead a charge as effectively as a group; (2) roles inevitably change in a building—for example, the stellar principal gets promoted or moved to a new school—and a team helps ensure the charge will continue despite the loss of any one person; and (3) sharing the pulpit is sometimes an effective strategy on its own—the reality is that the same message from the same messenger falls on deaf ears after a while.

Some districts and schools may have already created a data team, or school improvement team, to help make the shift into deeper conversations around data. School improvement teams or testing committees might be enhanced to become the 3D team. If your organization chooses to create a new team, it is imperative that it be assembled only after consulting with any existing groups with a similar charge. Nothing is more frustrating to already overtaxed educators than having a brand new task force created when current efforts might overlap. It is certainly not always necessary to build a new team, but if an existing team is transformed into a true 3D team, it is crucial that each member take part in ongoing professional conversations and exercises such as the ones in this book. In addition, the team leader must take a hard look at existing teams and make role changes if necessary to ensure efficiency, function, and varied representation.

Worksheet 1—A Broad Look at Your School or District led you to spend time reflecting on some important questions. Next, it's time to involve others in those issues and begin to set the stage for a truly data-driven organization.

The 3D Team's Charge

It is crucial that a group have a clear purpose. The focus of the 3D team is not simply to meet monthly around a table and talk about standardized test scores—although that can certainly be one worthwhile use of time. In the case of data-driven decision making, the group's purpose is to elevate conversations, enrich decisions, and inform the full school community. This team's goal is to lead the 3D charge, to start to influence the way conversations are held, and to form part of the base of the pyramid of school improvement. The 3D team is a group who helps remind others about positive change and asks questions about data integrity, cohesion of efforts, productive communications, and more.

When schools and districts establish a 3D team, the questions in Worksheet 2—The 3D Team's Charge should be asked right away. The team members leading this charge should be prepared to discuss these in an open and frank way. These questions, along with some typical responses, are presented as discussion starters and as an opportunity for group leaders to think ahead before diving in. Also, suggestions for data-related resources that might help a team get started are provided in Appendix B—Internet Resources.

3D Team Makeup

Any time a group is assembled whose charge is to push forth an agenda for comprehensive change, it is imperative that the group makeup be a true representation of the district or school. For example, a group in charge of technology planning that is made up only of "techies" will almost certainly be viewed by nontechies as noninclusive. Alternatively, a technology planning committee composed of teachers, parents, technology coaches, principals, media specialists, special education teachers, and students is in a far better position to truly represent the needs of a district.

Similarly, a 3D leadership team must consider representation from a variety of stakeholders, with careful consideration paid to ensuring a balanced mix of gender, cultural background, race, years of experience (including veteran educators and those new to the profession), grade level, content area, administrative experience, and so on. In addition, an objective parent as well as a local employer can be brought into the mix at relevant times to reduce bias. Finally, focused student representation should be interwoven at appropriate times, because students are, of course, the inspiration for all this work. We must be open to admitting that we don't know all the answers and that we haven't had all the experiences we might need. Bring in other folks with whom you might not have worked before. Denis Waitley, a productivity expert, once said, "You must look within for value, but must look beyond for perspective."

SCHOOL TEAM MEMBER CHECKLIST

There's no need to belabor a 3D team's makeup, but certainly more than a cursory thought should be given to ensuring appropriate representation using the details just discussed. At the school level, the principal is an understood, active member of this group and attends meetings, provides leadership, and ensures the championing of the entire school improvement culture.

Use Worksheet 3—School-Level Team Makeup to identify possible team members. Fill in the worksheet until you are confident that you have established a well-balanced team that will be inclusive enough to provide objective input and well-balanced conversations but small enough to be productive.

DISTRICT TEAM MEMBER CHECKLIST

At the district level, the superintendent becomes the de facto core of this group and attends meetings, provides leadership, and ensures the championing of the entire district improvement culture. The superintendent is also the one who ensures continuity of programs, budgets, and efforts and thwarts negative or unproductive feedback from other leadership staff.

Use Worksheet 4—District-Level Team Makeup to identify possible team members. Fill in the worksheet until you are confident that you have established a well-balanced team that will be inclusive enough to provide objective input and well-balanced conversations but small enough to be productive.

Teams within Teams

Many school improvement teams break down the work into manageable chunks and divvy out these chunks to smaller subgroups. These subgroups might include the following:

> **Data study**—ensures that every piece of data is considered, that a general understanding of critical data terms is established, and that each member understands the nuances of various summative reports. This subgroup would certainly need representation from a data coordinator or testing coordinator.

Central-office/school liaisons—works with department heads from the central office to discuss district issues, broader vision, professional development efforts, and resources.

Communications—presents findings to parent-teacher associations, booster clubs, community supporters, and school boards to help ensure that conversations outside school focus on "we're working on it" messages, and that communication isn't only one way.

Student input—members might have small focus groups from time to time with students to gain insight into student perceptions, obtain feedback on school climate, assess engagement levels with content areas, and so forth.

Moving Forward

When 3D teams decide to reach out and involve the whole school or district staff, it is imperative to have already worked out broad, flexible goals and to have made sure that district leadership staff are informed and committed. In addition, plans for involving the whole staff for any length of time should have been thought out to the point that detailed agendas, desired outcomes, times, and so forth are in place for at least the first few outreach meetings. This will help the team stay focused as this push begins.

Before venturing into actual data disaggregation, or focused school improvement planning based on standardized test data, it is critical to build a foundation by informing the whole group, engaging in dialogue about the bigger picture, and taking time to reflect on the solidity of the team as a whole. This culture building is a critical prerequisite to ensure team unity. A team that meets in an ongoing, focused way is also more likely to be able to carry school improvement work forward when administration changes.

The first few staff meetings should be aimed at setting the stage for a data-driven mindset.

Staff Meeting One: The Big Picture—Inform the whole group about the effort; include justification, goals, background, and a short professional reading on the topic of data-driven decision making as "homework" in preparation for the next meeting.

Staff Meeting Two: The Basics of 3D—Provide opportunities for staff to react to the previously presented information and the professional reading, as well as sharing additional information on the basics of data-driven decision making and how this approach fits into an overall school improvement mindset.

Staff Meeting Three: Team Building and Collaboration—Present a chance for the whole staff to dig deeper into the data, discuss trends, and reflect on the strengths and priorities for the staff as a whole.

Agenda ideas and suggestions for each staff meeting to help get you started are provided in the next three sections. By no means are these materials meant to be scripts or absolutes, but rather starting templates to get teams headed in the right direction. The 3D team should customize the meetings to the needs of the organization, outcomes of discussions, and goals of the effort. Once the foundation is in place, conversations might become more informal, be held in smaller groups, or be part of a bigger picture of staff development.

STAFF MEETING ONE—THE BIG PICTURE

As districts or schools choose to take on a more formal approach to data-driven conversations and practices, time must be spent looking at the big picture in addition to individual student performance measures. Leadership staff members within the school and district office must each agree that change of this nature occurs only when all players are on board, speaking the same message and committing their time and resources equitably and toward the same vision.

School staff members must begin to think in terms of what information has taken them to a particular path in instruction, curriculum development, re-teaching, and team planning. At the district level, regular cabinet meetings in which data and school performance issues are at the core of professional development efforts, grant writing endeavors, and improvement initiatives of any sort must become the norm. District staff must each agree that in order to create sweeping change, every effort, no matter how small, must concretely take into consideration the district vision and historic and current school performance challenges as well as improvement targets.

Further, every player must ask, "How might my actions affect others, and who should be a part of my current planning efforts? If I'm starting a new initiative, have I been careful to ask around and make sure someone else isn't doing something similar? How might my efforts best mesh with the efforts of someone else?" It is quite common to find very similar initiatives emerging from disconnected departments in school districts. Schools and districts in which each department communicates openly and frequently regarding their efforts, funding, and time are much more inclined to get the most return on their investments of time and money.

At the first meeting, identifying and sharing key components of the effort is important. Those components may include:

- Defining true data-driven decision making

- Exploring the concept of this idea as a culture, rather than an initiative

- Justifying the new mindset of data-informed decisions

- Setting overall goals

- Planning for feedback from staff and other participants in an ongoing way

- Providing a professional reading on data-driven decision making

Right from the start, it's important to make sure that each person understands that they do, in fact, have a clear role in a data-informed organization. Scott McLeod provides a well-written white paper that paints a picture of data-driven decisions across multiple layers of the education community. Find it here: www.hhsmckean.com/HHS_McKean/Social_Studies_links_files/ThoughtLeaders_DDDM_May05.pdf.

I would suggest that at this first meeting, in which you have decided to lay the groundwork for a more data-informed mindset, you have attendees read McLeod's white paper. Ask each participant to be prepared at the next meeting to discuss, reflect, and consider concrete items to address. Use Worksheet 5—Data-Driven Teachers to guide your discussion.

STAFF MEETING TWO—THE BASICS OF 3D

Use an idea flow chart (Figure 2.1) to facilitate a discussion encouraging staff to examine some decisions recently made at the school or central office. Ask each person to reflect aloud with the group any decisions that affected them in some way or that they were aware of. Topics might include the school calendar, schedule adjustments, teacher load, student council meeting times, athletic practice dates, and so on. Focus the discussion on simply naming decisions that have been made from any angle. This provides a chance for everyone to see a visual of just how many decisions get made in a short amount of time. Using a tool such as Inspiration (www.inspiration.com), Bubbl.us (http://bubbl.us), or Gliffy (www.gliffy.com) is a quick and easy way to coordinate this activity and provides a compelling visual to display just how many decisions are made on a regular basis.

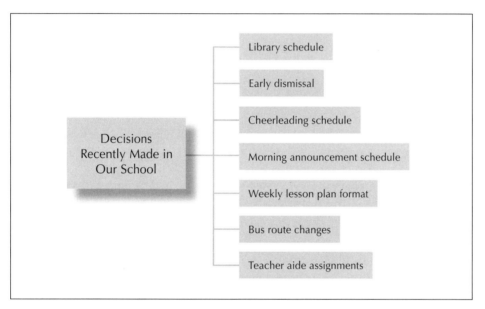

Figure 2.1. Chart decisions made to see ripple effects.

Being able to see a chart with multiple decisions, no matter how small they may seem, makes us pay closer attention to any ripple effect these decisions might have on the classroom and on teacher and student performance. 3D team members may begin to reflect on how these decisions were made or wonder why they were not involved. A decision made by a small group in the building often may fail to take into account other staff and events that it may affect. Getting into the habit of thinking further out, encompassing a virtual net across the school, allows us to be a little more "big picture" about the things we do and the effect we may be having on other areas.

Pick one of the decisions from the preceding activity, and dig a little deeper into the data surrounding that decision. Some districts and schools use a chart like the one shown in Figure 2.2 in their school improvement manuals and lesson plan books to present another chance to think "bigger picture" about the decisions that are made. District offices might be encouraged to print out poster-sized blank template charts and place them in the administrative meeting rooms as a visual aid when working on district-wide efforts.

Start with a current initiative at the core. Ask participants to respond with who and what might be affected by decisions on this topic. What does this initiative impact, and how? Will it affect student schedules? Does the issue need to be taken to the school board for consideration? Will this decision have an impact on funding? Will it affect teachers' time in the classroom? Keep these conversations going in an effort to reinforce how far-reaching every decision we make is, and how that makes it imperative that we don't make decisions without looking at various sources of data.

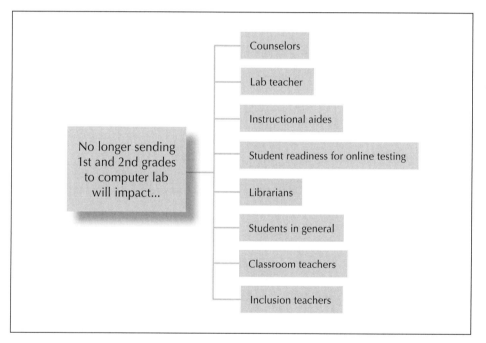

Figure 2.2. Choose one decision and dig in.

Finally, review key concepts from the McLeod white paper shared at Staff Meeting One. Ask these questions: What stood out? Does this article reflect your thoughts on data's role in your specific job? Does our organization follow this model?

STAFF MEETING THREE—TEAM BUILDING AND COLLABORATION

In the first two staff meetings, you introduced the concept of a more data-informed culture and provided opportunities for staff to discuss a more refined definition of data beyond simply test scores. In addition, these were both opportunities for participants to discuss their roles in data-driven decision making and to reflect on decisions already being made.

Before achieving a deeper, data-informed state of mind, district-level staff who were involved in creating and delivering professional development might have created workshops on topics of interest to them, or those they thought would garner the most attendance. For example, a science coordinator may have spent much of the year planning, acquiring, and developing a series of workshops on using microscopes because he or she saw these tools at a conference and thought they might have a valuable place in classrooms. Technology coordinators may have spent an entire summer delivering how-to workshops on the latest version of Web 2.0 tools, without much thought as to how the ultimate expertise of the participants might be connected to school performance and student needs.

This type of training should be replaced or enriched by more authentic, data-informed, ongoing professional learning efforts involving the whole school community. Central-office staff members who are responsible for planning professional development must look across the entire district office and actively seek out other departments to ensure alignment. They must work toward maximizing the outcome of workshops and more extended professional learning opportunities.

Time is of the essence in teachers' lives, so considering the details of why, when, and how to create and deliver professional development is of utmost importance. The collective intelligence of a well-integrated group of curriculum directors, technology specialists, special education coordinators, and others can enrich a professional development effort far beyond the traditional means. However, old habits are hard to break. We tend to work in silos. We must be proactive in seeking others out and including them in compelling ways to ensure that our efforts provide the maximum experience for all of our teachers. Looking out across our team from time to time, ensuring that we are seeking input from all key players, is just one important component of data-informed decision making.

Grant writing is another example in which we sometimes operate in an isolated way. One department within a school discovers a grant opportunity that sounds interesting. The grant is written, submitted, and received, and only then do other departments find out about it. At that point, it should not surprise anyone if uninvolved parties aren't as enthusiastic as we'd like them to be.

Highly effective school- and district-level teams work concretely to ensure integration and unity across content areas and grade levels. This requires that brainstorming meetings, planning meetings, and school improvement teams be truly integrated by engaging other school staff at all stages of development. An efficient, coherent, and successful school team plans with consideration given to each grade
level and department.

Use Worksheet 6—School-Level Collaboration Reflection and Worksheet 7—District-Level Collaboration Reflection to lead a discussion aimed at getting staff to consider the extent to which they include others in their planning efforts. They should do some reflection on the degree to which they consider the impacts of their efforts. This activity can be a good step in strengthening a team and raising awareness of team efforts. Many times we are surprised that we regularly leave people out of our conversations or plans simply by oversight. Consider printing these charts on poster paper as well, as a constant reminder to encourage us to think big picture and team unity each time a decision is made.

Encouraging the Culture

Using a concrete tool—one that gives us something tangible to work with—increases the chances that we'll break old habits. We are more likely to reach out to other departments with a plan in front of us. However, the traditional "inside the four walls of my classroom" way of thinking has permeated schools and districts for years, simply because of the nature of school structures.

The stakes are high now, and if the goal is to work toward an open culture of collaboration and a broader definition of data, we must plan to model this way of thinking. A superintendent who says to her cabinet, "I feel confident leading the district, and developing system-wide school improvement plans, but I don't feel that I am able to recognize curriculum alignment as well as some of you," sets the tone for everyone to be able to be recognized for their strengths, and respected for their willingness to accept the "lifelong learning" way of thinking. District staff members who don't feel confident asking for help or reaching out to others for input will have trouble adopting a truly data-informed way of working. Each of us has the responsibility to begin to implement this new way of thinking by stepping outside our comfort zone to practice what we preach. To consider, at the onset, how our efforts can influence, and be influenced by, other members of our school or district team is an important component of a data-enriched school culture.

As you begin to move ahead with additional faculty and staff outreach meetings and gain more focus on your efforts, it is important to be sure that the key players talk-the-talk and walk-the-walk. As you read earlier, the first few meetings of a 3D team should be spent getting into the mindset of taking more data-informed action. Modeling and informing others that this 3D team is basing meetings, goals, planning, and outreach efforts on informed conversations and school/district connectedness is crucial. In addition, leaders must epitomize a new, more open form of discussion. By engaging in an activity such as the Collaboration Reflection (Worksheet 6) and sharing the results of that conversation, one can encourage others to reflect on the connectedness of their own efforts.

In *Data Analysis for Continuous School Improvement* (2004, Eye on Education), Victoria Bernhardt uses the phrase "data safety and transparency." By this, she suggests that all the elements of data should be put out on the table and opened for viewing and scrutiny, and that the discussions surrounding this data should be nonthreatening for the participants. District leadership staff must be able to delve into data, track historical performance issues, and pull those issues out for greater examination. Coupled with that must be the "we're all in this together" attitude. Leading discussions about data that pinpoint specific areas of concern, without pointing fingers, sets the tone for safe data discussions and allows everyone involved to let down their guard, ask for help, and be more willing to seek input along the way.

Leading in 3D

A rule of thumb for leadership staff in ensuring that data-driven decision making isn't thought of as "just another initiative" is to ensure that each effort is carefully considered and all the options are weighed. Central office and administrative staff should model this data-informed mindset in ways that show they are clearly asking reflective questions for each decision of significance.

Depending on your role, and the role you are assuming in leading this effort, you may need to reframe the way you approach decisions and encourage others to do the same. Worksheets 8–14 provide examples of typical school and district decisions that need to be made concerning administrative leadership, professional development, grant writing, technology, curriculum design and alignment, finance, operations, and parent and community involvement.

Speaking the Same Language

Another key component for solidifying a more data-enriched way of operating is ensuring that data and improvement-related vocabulary is used correctly and consistently across districts and schools. Many districts have an official testing coordinator. The coordinator is very savvy about reading test scores, preparing test schedules, and reporting results to the Department of Education. In addition, most testing coordinators are quite knowledgeable about which tests are best for measuring which areas of success, and which areas in the district stand out as strong or troublesome. Although these testing coordinators provide one of the most valuable services in a district or school, if they are the only ones who speak the assessment and data language, there is sure to be a lack of clarity and uniformity. Further, if there are discrepancies between what the data coordinator thinks should be happening and what the teachers are actually doing in the building, this misalignment could cause major problems across the district or school.

It is very important to educate staff and the educational community as a whole about data vocabulary, general testing issues, progress measures specific to the schools, and formative and summative assessment definitions. Being proactive in ensuring there is a consensus on the accepted definitions of certain terms and using those terms uniformly in communications is a must.

Use the Glossary in Appendix A as a basis for data-related terminology that should be commonly understood and consistently communicated. Take steps to integrate these definitions and terminology into existing informative efforts such as parent newsletters, websites, and other communications.

WORKSHEET **2**

The 3D Team's Charge

1. What exactly is the purpose of the 3D team, and what is it hoping to accomplish?

    (Sample answer: Every school and district should always be working toward more enlightened conversations and decisions based on a better understanding of the overall picture of data. This group can help establish that mindset. We feel fragmented as an educational group right now, and we need a way to refocus and align our efforts.)

2. How often does the 3D team need to meet?

    (Sample answer: Our 3D team will meet once a week to begin, depending on what conditions are in place, time availability, etc., then move to biweekly meetings.)

3. What's the life cycle of the 3D team?

    (Sample answer: Preferably there is no "end" to this kind of culture, or to these conversations. Group members may come and go, and group structure may change, but the effort itself needs to be ingrained into the culture of the school. We are thinking we could eventually replace or refine our regular staff meetings to be focused on data and improvement conversations.)

4. What does the 3D team need to get started?

    (Sample answer: We need this team to have an awareness of the bigger data and student performance issues in the building(s). We also need to read some data-related articles as background.)

WORKSHEET 3

School-Level Team Makeup

MEMBER CATEGORY	NAME	REPRESENTS (or brings expertise from the perspective of) . . .
Principal		
Technology Leader		
Media Specialist		
Special Education Teacher		
Math Teacher		
Science Teacher		
Social Studies Teacher		
PE/Health Teacher		
Board Member		
Guidance Counselor		
Title I/Special Programs		
Student		
Parent		
Other		

WORKSHEET 4

District-Level Team Makeup

MEMBER CATEGORY	NAME	REPRESENTS (or brings expertise from the perspective of) . . .
Superintendent		
Assistant Superintendent		
Special Education Coordinator		
Technology Leader		
Media/Library Coordinator		
Testing/Data Coordinator		
Special Education Coordinator		
Content/Curriculum Leaders		
Board Member		
State Department of Education Liaison		
Guidance Counseling		
Title I/Special Programs		
Student		
Parent		
Other		

WORKSHEET 5

Data-Driven Teachers

Read the following white paper:

"Data-Driven Teachers" by Scott McLeod available at:
www.hhsmckean.com/HHS_McKean/Social_Studies_links_files/
ThoughtLeaders_DDDM_May05.pdf

Think about the following questions as you read the white paper:

- What forms of data do you use most often to make instructional or other decisions?

- Do you feel comfortable with exploring other forms of data?

- Is there unfamiliar terminology used?

- What "chunk" of data would you like to see that you don't currently have access to?

- What statements from the white paper are most thought-provoking?

- Are there any specific notions you would like to discuss as a large group?

WORKSHEET **6**

School-Level Collaboration Reflection

Each 3D team member in the building should consider how well his or her efforts integrate with others. After completing this activity initially as a 3D team, the results can be shared with the entire staff as a way to model the breaking down of silos.

DIRECTIONS:

Choose a recent or current team task or initiative (Are you considering writing a grant? Did you plan a grade-level field trip? Are you coordinating a multi-grade-level thematic unit?). Use the chart below to reflect on the extent to which you actively consider each of the grades/departments listed when you plan efforts. Modify the chart as needed. Check yourself using a ✓ or an X, to mark your efforts.

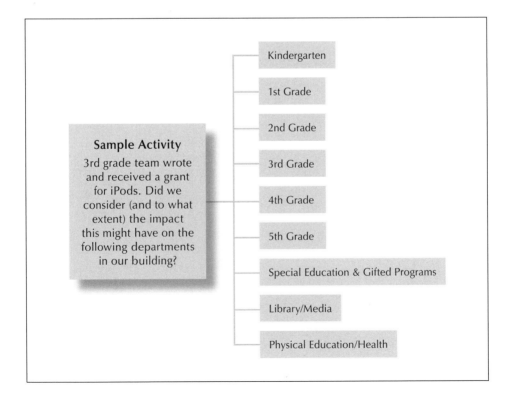

WORKSHEET 7

District-Level Collaboration Reflection

Each 3D team member in the district should consider how well his or her efforts integrate with departments. After completing this activity initially as a 3D team, the results can be shared with the entire staff as a way to model the breaking down of silos.

DIRECTIONS:

Choose a recent or current team task or initiative (Are you considering writing a grant? Did you plan a district-wide professional development offering? Are you coordinating a multi-grade curriculum redesign?). Use the chart below to reflect on the extent to which you actively consider each of the other departments listed when you plan and make decisions. Modify the chart as needed. Check yourself using a ✓ or an X, to mark your efforts.

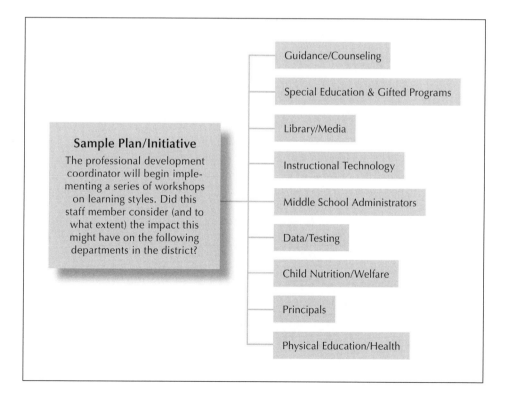

Sample Plan/Initiative

The professional development coordinator will begin implementing a series of workshops on learning styles. Did this staff member consider (and to what extent) the impact this might have on the following departments in the district?

- Guidance/Counseling
- Special Education & Gifted Programs
- Library/Media
- Instructional Technology
- Middle School Administrators
- Data/Testing
- Child Nutrition/Welfare
- Principals
- Physical Education/Health

WORKSHEET **8**

Administrative Leadership

- As Superintendent (or Assistant, or Principal), do I ensure a system of checks and balances across department heads?

- Do I ask section leaders why certain initiatives are being pushed, and how they are connected to the overall vision?

- Do I enable and encourage a team in which each player is intentional in involving other players?

- Do I make sure I personally take part in professional development, in addition to requiring it of others?

- Do I ensure that each department involves other key staff members who might not traditionally be included?

- Are budgeting decisions informed by data?

- Is the organizational structure—staff, scheduling, policy—aligned with our needs and vision?

WORKSHEET 9

Professional Development

- Does the professional development plan address specific areas of need beyond just summative test score data?

- Are our planned series of workshops concretely aligned to all various content areas?

- Why was a particular series of workshops chosen over another?

- Who was involved in the planning of these workshops?

- What specific student outcomes will this training eventually impact?

- Are these outcomes an area of note in our summative and formative test score data?

- How do we ensure that teachers are able to implement and formatively assess what they're being asked to do?

- Do teachers have access to ongoing, quality professional development that extends beyond basic workshops?

- Does someone monitor what professional development teachers have access to and take part in, to ensure that those teachers with performance issues are receiving the help and guidance they need?

- Why this topic? Why now?

Grant Writing

- How have we determined which areas are of highest priority?

- If our grant sources are limited, how have we decided as a whole district that this particular pursuit is the one that might be most beneficial?

- Has every single department been notified that we are pursuing this grant?

- Has a timeline been set so that each department understands their commitments, deadlines, and so on?

- Have their roles been defined?

- Has an evaluation plan been designed at the onset, and an evaluation team been established during the development of this grant?

- What measures has this team determined to be indicators of success?

- Can we continue this effort once grant funds are no longer available?

Technology

- Does the distribution of computers and other related technologies ensure equal and equitable access, beyond the simple classroom computer ratio count?

- Has professional development been considered before purchase?

- Who is providing this professional development?

- How is it connected to existing professional development offerings?

- Is this technology completely woven throughout each of the district's major departments?

- Have both the instructional and technical sides of things been considered, and have staff members from each of these departments been given equal consideration?

- Is this technology being purchased with the hope of affecting student achievement? How so? What components must be in place in order for this to happen?

- How will we determine consistency of use?

- What are the minimum expectations for teachers, students, and so on in regard to how this technology will be used?

Curriculum Design and Alignment

- Are teachers well-versed in assessment vocabulary?

- Are teachers provided professional development on formative assessment techniques?

- Do teachers clearly understand the connection between formative assessment and curriculum standards? How about between summative assessments and curriculum?

- How do we ensure that what our teachers are teaching is truly aligned with content standards?

- How do we help teachers connect assessments to what is actually being taught?

- Is our district-wide curriculum vertically aligned to ensure that standards progress logically from grade to grade?

- Can we identify any gaps?

- Are our principals trained in how to help teachers with formative assessment?

WORKSHEET 13

Financial and Operations

- Can we logically connect expenditures to our student achievement goals? Is that realistic? If not, how are we justifying expenditures?

- Are financial decision makers concretely involved in curricular meetings to ensure they understand why budgets are designed the way they are?

- Are finance-related policies established (or restructured when necessary) to support revised efforts in curriculum, instruction, and student learning?

- Is the business office a player in curricular aspects of the division?

- Is the mission of finance and operations departments written with student learning as the ultimate goal?

WORKSHEET **14**

Parental and Community Involvement

- Do parents receive feedback on their child's progress in a timely manner?

- Do parents receive updates on the school's overall progress on an ongoing basis?

- Do we proactively report good news to our community and educate them on how to become more involved with the learning process?

- Have we educated our parents and community on how schools have changed and what 21st-century skills look like?

- Have we created unique opportunities in which to reach our parents (webinars, text messaging, etc.)?

- Do parents understand how homework might look drastically different from when they were in school? Do they understand why? Have we given them assistance on how they might best help at home?

3

Examining the Data and Issues

WE'VE SET the wheels in motion to focus our conversations around data and synchronize our staff efforts. We've reflected on the fact that data-informed district efforts must take into consideration all the critical stakeholders. Further, we've agreed to use a common set of terms when speaking and dealing with data in order to help tighten our direction and efforts. This chapter will provide numerous staff development templates and suggestions for enlightening a school, group of schools, or district office to the key points of examining data consistently and uniformly.

Once we've initiated this process of committing to a more data-informed way of working and begun to solidify our commitment to a more focused district- or school-wide team, we must examine our various layers of data with a more purposeful intent. What does our student performance data tell us? What performance differences do we notice among our various student populations? What connections can we make between this performance and the school environment? If we are truly trying to solve data issues, what resources and professional development efforts are in place to help? Questions such as these must be asked on a continuous basis each time we have additional data to investigate.

For years, many schools and districts have administered standardized tests and used the resulting information to look at major gains or dips in student performance. Many teachers would receive test results in the fall from a test administered to a different group of students from the prior spring. Although this data proved helpful, little professional development was available to make good use of the information. Further, many teachers had little training or knowledge regarding *formative* assessment opportunities. A school test coordinator might spend some time reviewing classroom and grade-level aggregate data to determine key strengths and weaknesses, but little was done in the way of pulling out performance trends and making changes in curriculum and instruction to address those trends. Finally, teachers might have been able to glance over classroom and student test printouts and make note of areas that stood out, but most were not schooled in the fine art of test score analysis.

Schools and districts are realizing now, however, that everyone involved in education must be able to read and explore formative and summative assessment information, recognize areas of strength and concern, and, through a network of educators around us, receive help in making necessary adjustments in instruction and curriculum design on an ongoing basis. Although this workbook is not designed to guide one through the process of psychometrics, this chapter will provide practical tools and templates for working with the big picture of a data-informed effort. Most standardized testing companies offer numerous data analysis tools and guides to help users understand all the technical terms involved in school performance data. This handbook doesn't delve into the technical side of analyzing means, medians, stanines, and the like. However, familiarity with those concepts is a must in preparing a solid palette of data tools and knowledge. For additional tools and templates, visit Scott McLeod's School Data Tutorials website (http://schooltechleadership.org/research/school-data-tutorials/).

The School Improvement Mechanic

When speaking to staff who are new to a data-driven approach, it is important to frame conversations in practical ways. Staff might consider approaching performance data in the same way we would want a mechanic to approach our car after it starts making an odd or abnormal noise. We take our car to a mechanic and tell her about the noise. If she were to take the car, *without asking any additional questions*, and tell us she'll have the problem fixed shortly, we'd be concerned. How would we know that our car will be better off after the service call? One would hope she'd probe a little more and ask a series of questions like:

- What does the noise sound like?
- When exactly does the noise occur?
- Does it happen every time you drive?
- Can you pinpoint the location of the noise?
- Does the noise get louder as you accelerate?
- How long has the car been making this noise?
- Does the noise occur in conjunction with braking?
- Does anyone else hear the noise besides you?

We need to put ourselves in the position of the data mechanic. We can gain immense insight into our functions if we ask layered questions like the ones just listed.

Similarly, if a parent received a report stating that his child was not performing up to par, we would hope he would be presented with a detailed explanation of any key terms, the short- and long-term impact of the child's performance, and a synopsis of what the school or district plan is to raise the performance.

Digging a few levels deeper into data than we've traditionally done in the past can be a very revealing exercise. Unfolding as many layers of school performance as possible and making connections among these layers paints a clear map and enables us to chart a course more successfully.

Root cause is typically defined as the most fundamental and underlying reason for a problem or issue. In terms of educational data, it means getting beyond a surface-level symptom and exploring down as far as one can go to get to something concretely addressable. If a teacher is told, for example, "You need to really work on your boys' math computation abilities," she hasn't been given much to go on. That directive is so overwhelming and global that it's difficult to formulate a plan of attack. However, if the teacher had been a part of multiple conversations about data where detailed consideration was given, we might reach something more addressable, such as, "We've found that the male students who failed the 'understanding sentence structure' portion of the reading test were the same students who scored poorly on the problem-solving portions of the math test." That thought gives us much more to go on and paints a clear picture of how one might go about dealing with this issue. It also gives us more information to help us figure out who can best help us solve this problem. Is it the principal, the math coordinator, a reading specialist?

As another example, a local administrator implemented a school-wide mandate in which seventh grade boys had to eat lunch in an area separate from the rest of the middle school because there were so many discipline issues with them at lunch. Because of this mandate, the cafeteria schedule had to be adjusted, the school schedule itself was altered, staff member planning time breaks were moved, and so on. Numerous changes were put into place without anyone giving consideration as to *why* the seventh grade boys had so many cafeteria-related discipline issues to begin with, or whether there was one subpopulation of seventh grade boys who were at the core of this issue. The end result was that cafeteria staff was now unhappy, teachers didn't like it, and, worst of all, the seventh grade boys as a whole were just as unruly in the new setting. The school had addressed only a symptom of a problem, instead of getting down to the root cause.

Why wasn't an impromptu team put together to explore this issue further? What was the deepest the staff could dig to determine why this subset of the population behaved the way they did? Was their behavior truly distinguishable from the other subpopulations? Numerous lenses could be used to examine this issue, before making a massive school-wide change that didn't produce a better situation.

Making Connections

Looking at data more deeply to recognize patterns of performance and trouble spots is an ongoing exercise. Being able to explore connections between various sources of data can help pinpoint root causes. For example, can we find out if the subgroup of students who score the lowest in the *Making Inferences* section of a standardized reading test might also have other similar test performance issues? Did these students all take part in the same remediation assistance the prior year? What about the students who score highest in *Math Reasoning*, for example? Do they take part in school enrichment activities of any kind?

Although it's true that not every angle can be investigated, key student performance issues certainly warrant in-depth consideration beyond one layer. Further, sometimes the most important discoveries cannot be made by looking at a single data set. Although a printout of a class aggregate of standardized test scores gives us great insight into how the class performed as a whole on portions of the test, it doesn't provide much guidance for making instructional changes. We must get into the habit of looking at ongoing data and considering nontraditional sources of information. We always think of test scores, demographics, absenteeism, and so on. But what else might have an impact on how our students are learning, or how successful our teaching efforts are? A 3D team might present the following series of activities as a way to encourage staff to consider all the various data that impacts the learning environment. Worksheet 15—Thinking Outside the Box encourages the whole group to think beyond traditional sources of data. After a few initial, large-group meetings that help start the flow in the right direction, subgroups can be formed to break off and examine data more closely.

Take a moment to read over the data presented in Worksheet 16—Data Conversation Activity 1. A cursory glance would tell you that the students performed better overall in *Informative Reading* than they did in *Extended Understanding*. Ask any layperson and they would say the same thing. You might also infer that overall the *Higher-Order Questioning* section has the fewest students performing above average. But is that really what this data tells us? Does data in this form help us at all at this point? If we're familiar with the testing items and what exactly they measure, perhaps it does. If we know the curriculum, how this test aligns to that curriculum, and how our own instruction mirrors this curriculum, we might have something to go on. For example, a district-level reading director might immediately begin to think of what standards in the curriculum match these test item categories. In that case, this data might be very helpful in thinking about performance across the district.

However, looking at a generic set of data without more refined headers or other information such as the actual number of items, or the weight given to each category, gives us only a very broad first look at what's going on. It's an important look, no doubt. But because there isn't much in this broad view that gives us something concretely addressable, it's critical that we not stop there.

Let's add a little more information and dig a little deeper into this data set. In Worksheet 17—Data Conversation Activity 2, we've separated males from females and shown the number of items tested. With raw, clean data that we are sure is accurate, we can make a quick table to examine things a little more closely. We also need to get into the habit of making sure the data we're viewing can provide answers to the questions we have.

A 3D team member leading a group through these activities might consider the following general questions with regard to the data as it is presented in Worksheet 17:

- Does this data appear to be accurate? How would we know?
- Would it matter if we knew how many students were tested?
- Can you tell if the number of males and females is equal? Does that matter?
- Is this data in a format that gives us enough information?
- Is this data in a format that is easily understandable?
- What further data do we need, if anything?
- What kinds of assumptions can we make with just the data presented here?
- Does every person in this school or department understand the data as presented?
- Do we all have the same assumptions?

Revisit the data after discussing the questions just listed, and think about these additional issues:

- Is one gender outperforming another overall?
- What specific differences do we see between male and female performance?
- If this chart presented the number of students tested, would that change our assumptions about the data presented here? Why or why not?
- What about differences in performance between subtests?
- To what extent is one group outperforming another?
- Is this difference significant enough to warrant further investigation?
- If we need to dig into this data more, where do we get additional, more detailed reports?

- Do these students belong to a certain homeroom?

- Can we identify specific students? Is there a need to do this?

- Might we look at this set of data side by side with the two previous years to see if there was growth? Decline?

- Do the scores here paint a complete and accurate picture of what students know? Of what teachers taught?

Even with the added information in the second set of data, we still may not be at the point to make a truly informed conclusion. Considering external factors, testing conditions, and other forms of assessment data might give us a clearer picture. Mixing in previous summative test performance, formative assessment data, and so on might allow us to feel more confident in making a judgment about this data set.

What other questions would you have at this point?

Data Conversations Continued

A next logical step in this series of conversations is to sit down with real performance data specific to schools and ask the same series of questions as in the previous section. A testing coordinator should be present to lead faculties or departmental teams through the questions and to get everyone looking at data with some leading questions in mind. This will also allow another opportunity to ensure that each staff member is using terminology correctly and is able to clarify any questions or concerns about what they're viewing. A principal and a curriculum-oriented staff person should also be present to help keep conversations focused and positive.

This would also be a good time to form breakout groups. One group of fifth grade teachers, along with a physical education teacher, counselor, and the district math coordinator, might go work on fifth grade data. The fourth grade group might enlist a fine arts teacher and an assistant principal. These breakout groups walk away with a charge to examine their grade-level data in light of the questions posed in the previous sections, then report back patterns, connections that they have uncovered, and other issues of note. Make sure that a 3D team member is present at each of these breakout groups to help ensure consistency of conversation and keep discussions on task. Agree on a clear direction, a timeline, and some general rules for reporting findings back to the larger group.

School Performance Interview Activity

Another way to begin an examination of data is to ask staff to give immediate responses to a specific school performance issue. In this conversation, you simply want to get a feel for what people currently think in regard to an issue. Be careful *not* to take action yet on assumptions or hasty responses to data issues. However, looking at how people react to a performance issue can provide some insight into whether the school or district as a whole thinks in unison about certain issues, or if certain team members have drastically differing views. Take one specific concern from your own data set you wish to investigate. Ask staff to give their thoughts on a data issue specific to the school. Let everyone speak, and pay attention to all contributions. Encourage the team to keep the conversation positive.

Here's an example. Say that a standardized assessment shows that seventh grade females significantly outperform males in reading comprehension sections A and D. As the staff gives feedback, you might get the following responses from teachers: "There are not enough supplemental materials to reinforce this skill." "Teachers have not been trained on how best to teach this skill. The professional development we went to last year didn't address this." "We were not informed that this item was being tested, so we did not spend much time on this." "Girls always do better in reading than boys anyway, so I don't think this is something we should worry that much about." And administrators might respond, "I'm not sure teachers were given enough professional development on the updated curriculum," or "I think we should probably look a little more closely to see if this is really true across the board. I can't imagine there's a great difference between the genders, generally speaking." Having a 3D team member lead these conversations can reinforce the focus on actual data and push staff to continue asking and digging until root causes are unearthed.

School Performance Interview Reflections

There are times when getting informal opinions on data is important. Concrete actions need not be taken on the feedback we gather initially, although it's certainly not a bad idea to keep these responses at hand when examining and planning for strategies to address specific problems down the road. Listening to how staff react to data and performance problems can be a good indicator of their understanding of key data terminology and can help inform necessary content in future meetings about data.

As a next step, choose *one* data issue and consider which staff members might have the most feedback regarding this issue *right away*. Who else besides classroom teachers might have insight? Should students be asked to give their thoughts? How about staff members from another school? How about parents? After you have gathered some insightful feedback, consider which responses might be pointing in the direction of a true root cause. Might we want to revisit those respondents to gather more information? Do we have data to support their claims? Which responses are *not* worth scrutinizing more closely, and why? What data sources beyond the interviews might inform this issue?

The 3D team can help take the generic examples provided here and substitute real data in their place. School leaders can help form data workgroups, whose charge it is to examine subsets of data, then report back to the whole faculty or to a larger data team. Leaders can also offer assistance either directly or by inviting key central-office personnel or other school faculty members to the table. It is important that a structure be put in place that continues these conversations either as replacements for traditional staff/faculty meetings or as a part of them. Some districts and schools choose to have a monthly schedule in which a member of the core 3D team facilitates focused discussions on short subsections of testing data. Others work with the central-office staff to get professional development on making better use of formative assessments.

Data Overlays

In *Data Analysis for Continuous School Improvement* (2004, Eye on Education), Victoria Bernhardt describes the process of using "multiple measures" of data to ensure that we see the broader and deeper picture of data as it relates to overall school improvement. She states, "Analyses of demographics, perceptions, student learning, and school processes provide a powerful picture that will help us understand the school's impact on student achievement. When used together, these measures give schools the information they need to improve teaching and learning and to get positive results."

Including multiple measures such as formative and summative assessment data, teacher professional development data, student attitudes, demographics, and other key data and then superimposing one data set over another (creating a "data overlay") can provide a fantastic way to make new hypotheses about school and student performance issues.

Refer back to the data set presented in Worksheets 16 and 17. What else might have impacted those performance scores? What if we looked at which teachers were tied to which students being tested? Are any of those students receiving special education assistance? What is the background of these students? Are bands of students who perform in some way all coming from the same teachers in prior years? Asking questions such as these helps us look beyond a performance number and get down to the classroom level in which we might be able to concretely address the root cause of a performance problem.

Possibilities for data overlays:

- Student reading scores disaggregated by male and female and attached to specific teacher names

- Individual student performance scores, with parental information included such as attendance at parent-teacher meetings or after-school enrichment activities

- Student behavior records coupled with test-score and schedule data

- Participation in a fine arts program, intersected with student attitudinal survey data

- Teacher professional development attendance records intersected with student subgroup performance

- Teacher degree and years of experience records coupled with student discipline information

Revisit the "School Improvement Mechanic" way of thinking on page 43. Asking another set of questions, followed by another, lets us get a little closer to the bottom line of performance. Worksheet 18—Layering Data Sets steps you through a simple example.

If you were able to look at summative test score data, aggregated by gender and race, and were then able to separate this data by teachers, would you be more informed? Probably. If you could make a connection between that data and those teachers' participation in districtwide professional development efforts, might that be one factor to help you make decisions about the success of this professional development? Absolutely!

Taking broad data sets at face value isn't unhelpful by any means. It provides a great starting point and an impetus for conversations. But without a deeper analysis, it only provides limited assistance. Taking the time to make solid connections between various data sets gives us a better table on which to operate.

Core Concepts

Although each staff member may play a different role in the overall data-informed organizational structure, there are certain core concepts that every staff member should be familiar with to have a solid foundation on which to work.

Every staff member should understand these core concepts:

- Basic Data Terminology (see Appendix A—Glossary)
- Data Sources
  - What are our various sources of data?
  - How do I access these data sets?
  - Who can help me access data?
  - Who is my first point of contact when I need help with data, assessments, and so on?
- Standardized Test Familiarity
  - Which tests measure what in our school?
  - At what grade levels are the various content areas tested?
  - How do our various tests determine our success?
- Requirements and Expectations
  - Where does our school/district stand in regard to meeting our growth goals?
  - Where are we headed specifically?
- Formative Assessment
  - Are my formative assessments telling me what I need to know?
  - Do I have strategies for using formative data?
  - What techniques do we use for development, delivery, analysis, and appropriate action?
  - Who leads curricular alignment?

3D teams might consider using a tool like The Advanced Learning Technologies' ProfilerPRO (http://profilerpro.com) to set up a self-assessment of data strengths and knowledge. This assessment tool is designed to analyze your organization's knowledge level against core competencies that you establish. It can be very useful in determining what kinds of knowledge building or professional development would most help to ensure a quality understanding of data concepts. It also provides a listing of "experts" in each category, thus clearly identifying peers across the school or district who could be called on for assistance.

For example, a 3D team might create a short survey in which staff members self-assess their current level of comfort with key data-informed core concepts such as the ones just listed. This can be used as a pre-assessment to identify breakout group leaders. In addition, it can serve as a midpoint check to (1) inform the 3D team about individual progress of staff members, and (2) model to staff members the importance of formative assessment to aid the team in making efficient progress.

The School Improvement Mechanic Model Revisited

Taking time to ask additional levels of *why, what, how, where,* and *when* can get us closer to discovering the true culprit behind data issues. For example, ask an overworked teacher why her students aren't performing up to par in math, and she may say, "Because kids don't pay attention like they did years ago." Ask her why that is, and she may say, "Because they are so multisensory that they can't just stay focused on the book like I tell them to." Are we satisfied that we've discovered the problem yet? No, there's more to uncover. What else might we want to ask, and how far do we need to dig until we get at least a little closer to what's happening? How can we possibly help this teacher if we stop at her first two responses? Do we want to know what her definition of "focused on the book" means? What if we observed her style of teaching? What if we examined which specific students she teaches? What if we were able to look at some patterns of formative assessment performance in this classroom? What if we could compare this year's scores to last year's and the ones from the year before? How do the students in her classroom perform in other content areas? Does our standard teacher observation system provide enough detail to paint a true picture of why students are performing the way they are? Of the resources made available to this teacher, which does she engage? Why those?

Taking a problem, asking deep, probing questions, and superimposing multiple sources of hard data enables us to determine the root cause(s) of the issue(s) at hand. Being able to identify a problem *at its core* can help us create and enact a tangible strategy to improve on the challenge, making us more certain that our strategy isn't just a Band-Aid for an issue that will continue to fester outside our scope of operation.

Most importantly, moving staff to a level at which each person is constantly in this data discovery, reflection, and action mode ensures that we continuously improve on existing successful efforts, streamline the hard work already being done, and exemplify what we strive to build in our students—lifelong learning.

Victoria Bernhardt in her book *Using Data to Improve Student Learning in Middle Schools* (2004, Eye on Education) notes that "Your best defense against others drawing incorrect or incomplete assumptions about your school is to provide a complete analysis" (p. 238).

Beginning to scrutinize data in new ways, and with new lenses, offers us the chance to finally heal previously hidden fractures that may have plagued our performance for years. Getting into the habit of asking additional questions *each and every time we look at data*, be it small ongoing formative measures, or district-level aggregate standardized test scores, increases the likelihood that we can get to the bottom of academic successes and performance discrepancies.

WORKSHEET **15**

Thinking Outside the Box

Brainstorm ways in which you might collect valuable data about your school or district performance. Think about other kinds of data you need or other ways you might want to look at existing data. What else would help you zoom in on, and be able to examine, a school performance issue? Start with the traditional "in the box" sets of data, such as aggregate test scores, but as you progress, think about how other data impacts what you do and how you grow as an organization.

List other sources of data you'd like to investigate.

List additional sources of data.

Think Outside the Box!

Standardized assessments	Teacher observations
Weekly tests	Parent surveys
9-Week tests	Attendance data
Group self-assessments	

Data Conversation Activity 1

Take a look at the following sample of district-level subset data. These scores represent district-level aggregate scores from a standardized reading test for sixth graders.

READING COMPREHENSION	% BELOW AVERAGE	% AVERAGE	% ABOVE AVERAGE
Initial Understanding	26	65	9
Vocabulary Reconstruction	22	58	20
Extended Understanding	45	45	10
Informative Reading	21	61	18
Higher-Order Questioning	30	64	6

List three things you infer from a cursory review of this data.

Data Conversation Activity 2

MALES

READING COMPREHENSION	# OF ITEMS TESTED	% BELOW AVERAGE	% AVERAGE	% ABOVE AVERAGE
Initial Understanding	8	20	69	11
Vocabulary Reconstruction	6	25	53	22
Extended Understanding	4	46	42	12
Informative Reading	1	22	60	18
Higher-Order Questioning	6	24	66	10

FEMALES

READING COMPREHENSION	# OF ITEMS TESTED	% BELOW AVERAGE	% AVERAGE	% ABOVE AVERAGE
Initial Understanding	8	24	53	23
Vocabulary Reconstruction	6	17	57	26
Extended Understanding	4	36	42	22
Informative Reading	1	19	61	20
Higher-Order Questioning	6	32	56	12

What are the key questions to ask at this point?

WORKSHEET 18

Layering Data Sets

Create a data overlay to help you see how data sets intersect by filling in the following chart. Add columns of data connections, one layer at a time, as in the example below. Creating a data overlay can help you identify patterns and see where to target your efforts.

Data Layer One	Data Layer Two	Data Layer Three	Data Layer Four	Data Layer Five

Example

Our 3D team would like to make connections between the following layers of data:

Student Summative Test Score Data	Student Attitudinal Survey Data	Classroom Discipline Infractions	Teacher Professional Development Records

What else might be considered? Do you have access to this data? Can you get access to this data?

4

Maximizing Technology's Role

TECHNOLOGY INTEGRATION and technical infra-structure play critical but different roles in a data-informed and successful educational culture. Highly effective instruction simply must include technology integration if it is genuinely aimed at improving the educational lives of students in the 21st century. Teachers must work hard to enrich the solid content and teaching strategies they employ with tools and opportunities that reflect the world outside school, and they must provide avenues for students to go beyond standardized measurements. School leaders must ensure that they walk-the-walk in regard to emphasizing technology's role. Further, it is imperative that leadership staff work to provide the resources, training, and support to enable teachers to use technology in effective ways that reach out to every single student.

A solid technology infrastructure helps bridge opportunities between these instructional efforts and the need to ensure that those efforts are based on relevant, timely, and accurate data. A data management system or warehouse can offer a streamlined way for staff to have ongoing access to information to help them make the right choices and continuously improve the opportunities for students. Data software and utilities that can quickly summarize, aggregate, and disaggregate data are powerful instruments in the toolbox of school improvement. Being comfortable enough and knowledgeable enough to ask the right questions about data is fundamental. Having powerful and easy-to-use tools at our disposal that can quickly provide answers is equally important.

Integration and Access

Conversations around technology integration are less and less about "how-to" training and more about an instructionally focused approach that more clearly targets an ultimate goal of instructional growth. This continues to be the aim of most professional development related to instructional technology. Technology integration in the old sense, in which lessons were taught and technology was considered an add-on to integrate later, is losing ground to a more authentic use of technology in which it is a genuine and truly interwoven piece of the learning environment.

Students from the past 20 or so years have now graduated and are active members of a booming digital life thanks in no small part to our use of technology in the classroom. They are voting digitally, banking online, and living in a world well integrated with technology. The students of today don't need lengthy lessons on how to use a mouse. They don't need a workshop on how to use a cell phone or send a text message. Their lives are heavily digital. Many students entering school now assume that our classrooms will provide them easy access to information and digital technologies.

THE INTERNAL DIGITAL DIVIDE

If some of our students have access to digital resources such as high-speed Internet and communication devices at home, and some do not, then our *primary opportunity to level the technology playing field is in school*. Therefore, it is critical that we look at the use of technology across the entire district and conduct a scan of the landscape to see if we are in fact providing digitally equitable learning environments for every student we serve. Because numerous books are available that deal with the how-to of technology integration, as well as administrative technology standards and use, this section will explore technology use from a few other angles.

First, I would argue that those teachers who truly *want* to integrate technology are already doing it. Although technology access certainly isn't overflowing across every classroom in the country, for the most part we're somewhat beyond the older barriers of not having the "stuff" yet. I am well aware that many classrooms still struggle to get the equipment they need at the level they desire. But I do think that access has improved over time. My informal observations of classrooms where technology is *not* being integrated well have to do more with the teacher not yet being convinced of technology's critical importance or the administrator not establishing technology integration as the norm. Many of us have probably heard a teacher say, "My test scores are fine, I'm good at classroom management, so I don't feel like I really need to worry about technology stuff." No one can discount adequate test scores and good classroom management, but if that's the only target we're reaching for in our classrooms, then our future workforce is in serious trouble. Good classroom management and adequate test scores are the floor level of attainment, not the ceiling. The director of human resources at a large corporation relayed the following story to me:

> Years ago, ACT scores, GPAs, and resume bullets were what I looked at in potential employee applications. I have learned over time that those only paint part of the picture. While I need basic intelligence and a certain body of knowledge in the people I hire, what I really want is someone who can thrive in the 21st-century workforce. That means, I can plop them down in the middle of a group in the midst of a current work problem. They can interact with the group, ask relevant questions, and immediately go to a computer and other sources and start researching information. They should then be able to turn that information around in a short time, and present findings or strategies back to me. I don't care if they don't know the factual answers. But if they don't know how to be a productive part of a conversation, use a multitude of digital resources to look for an answer, then come back and prepare and present potential solutions, they are of no help to me in this company. Someone who *can* do those things is immensely more helpful than someone with good test scores.

What this says to me is that the "I've got good test scores and my students behave" idea is merely a fraction of the overall instructional environment. Although having good test scores might help a classroom or school meet an annual school improvement measure, it only carries so much weight in the real world outside school. An environment in which technology is seamlessly interwoven throughout the culture of a school helps us provide more to our students than "adequate" yearly progress. Who wouldn't agree that we want more for our students than just adequate?

This puts pressure on the entire school system to look a little more closely at which classrooms are truly integrating the use of technologies into the classroom. It means we must update our definitions of effective technology integration. It means we must think beyond remedial labs through which we funnel our students in an effort to prepare them for standardized tests. Multimedia production, presentations, research, and authentic uses of science equipment, journaling, and problem solving of all kinds must be the norm. Capitalizing on the social nature of Web 2.0 tools can only help us better reflect the real world outside school. As a 3D leadership team, we must be strategic in our efforts to further enrich the classrooms where technology integration is the norm. We must be deliberate and intentional in our efforts to push forward those classrooms where "adequate" is a goal. Just as we measure growth in our students by a battery of standardized tests, we must measure progress in our use of technology in at least a moderately quantifiable way as well.

MEASURING TECHNOLOGY USE

We live and work in the age of "that which gets measured, gets done." Years ago, a noted measure of technology readiness and success was the achievement of a specific computer-to-student ratio and an acceptable level of Internet connectivity. Policies around the world established this measure as a key indicator by which schools and districts received funding and support. This push to increase access was a huge effort and made new and improved learning environments possible. Many schools and districts went above and beyond ratios of connectivity and focused additionally on professional development to make sure teachers and others were able to use this technology appropriately and effectively. Technology connections, access, and increased expertise made new things possible and removed barriers that existed before.

If we want to advance classroom environments, we must be deliberate in tracking and making progress and helping teachers realize our expectations. I would not at all suggest that measuring technology use is an easy task, or one to which we can apply the same scientific rigor we would in a nonhuman environment. We can, however, have concrete expectations for where we want our classrooms to be academically through the effective use of technology, and we can observe progress toward that goal. We can have meaningful conversations and staff development that paints a picture beyond the merely adequate.

Using a baseline summary questionnaire, needs assessment, or survey that describes our current state of technology integration is a good way to start. Conducting a survey of an individual school, a group of administrators, or a central office can help you determine the attitudes, beliefs, and skills around technology integration. Understanding their current thoughts on the use of technology will enable you to factor in what kinds of support or guidance they may need to reach the district's 21st-century vision for its classrooms. Administering this kind of assessment to central-office staff, principals, and teachers should be step one.

The ProfilerPRO utility (http://profilerpro.com) is a valuable tool you could use to create and manage needs assessments. The free version allows users to create and conduct basic surveys to use for school improvement. You'll find numerous technology integration surveys, some already aligned to ISTE's National Educational Technology Standards.

I recommend that schools and districts think *broadly* about the use of technology in the school(s) to help gather this set of data for overall school improvement. Here are key questions to consider:

Teachers:

- To what extent is technology well integrated across your discipline?

- Is every single student in your classroom afforded the same opportunity to use technology in meaningful ways?

- Does your administration encourage and enable you to experiment with new and emerging technologies—that is, Web 2.0 tools, student multimedia production, or global communication and collaboration opportunities?

- What barriers prohibit you from using technology in more meaningful ways?

- What concrete help is needed to push technology use in your classrooms to an extent that mirrors the technology-driven world outside school?

Principals:

- Do you have a clear understanding of technology's important role in moving beyond adequate test scores?

- How do you advance this agenda with every single staff person in the building?

- How do you actively model its importance?

- How confident are you that graduates of your school are workforce-ready?

Central-Office Staff:

- Do we share the same vision for what technology can do to ensure that our district exceeds adequate yearly progress?

- Is this vision reflected in all of the professional development efforts we offer to our teachers, regardless of which department coordinates these offerings?

- What policies and procedures are in place that certify technology's use in such a way that is equitable and legitimate across the district?

- What professional development are we attending that keeps us at the forefront of 21st-century education?

TECHNOLOGY SCANS

After discussing some broad questions, schools and districts may want to dig a little deeper and get a more detailed feel for technology's role in the learning and teaching process. Conducting a more formal needs assessment of your school(s) may provide useful data that:

- Identifies areas of need in regard to access, connectivity, resources, and professional development requests;

- Shows spots across a grade level in which technology may not be being used effectively;

- Highlights sections of the various content areas in which technology *is* used well;

- Offers an opportunity to come to consensus across a building about the vision for technology and an agreed-upon definition of "true technology integration"; and

- Provides concrete data on which to make technology decisions in relation to purchases, professional development, filtering and policy issues, and so on.

Technology scans (or audits, as they are sometimes called in the more formal scope) can help to answer two questions: What do we have? And how well are we using what we have? Having more tangible data about these two issues can help teachers, principals, technology coordinators, and other decision makers ensure that time, money, and efforts are well spent—in other words, that technology-related decisions are data-driven!

A simple instructional technology inventory can provide a nice baseline for what equipment, supplies, resources, and connectivity are in place. Use Worksheet 19—Instructional Technology Checklist 1: What Do We Have? and Worksheet 20—Instructional Technology Checklist 2: How Well Are We Using What We Have? to assess your integration-related access, equipment, and resources.

Data Warehousing

Most schools and districts have enormous amounts of data all over the place. Individual teachers have sets of data. Schools have sets of data that feed into central-office databases. Central-office databases feed into state department databases, and so on. Sometimes this flow works well; however, many times these databases are not in sync. There are kinks in the way each set of data "talks" to another set, and humans have to step in and check the integrity of data as it passes from one system to another. This can cause serious lag times, for example, when a teacher keeps individual cumulative paper cards with student information and this information has to be manually transferred to and from numerous places.

Schools and districts that begin to realize the power of data also soon realize the need for having all these data sets coordinated in a central and focused, technology-enabled way. This is typically referred to as a *data warehouse*. A data warehouse is the central computerized storage area where the data from all the sources comes together. Each entity within the organization simply pushes and pulls from this central core of data as needed. With an efficient, streamlined data warehouse, each person who might need to access data has the ability to pull just the pieces of data required to perform the task at hand. This central core of data is protected from being jeopardized either intentionally or unintentionally. Using a data warehouse system helps to prevent overlap, infidelity between data sets, and inefficiency as a whole. Budget meetings and technology-planning sessions should use a formal checklist (see Worksheets 21 and 22) when initiating a data warehouse to help focus questions and inform the larger conversation of data planning.

Privacy and security issues can be handled easily and efficiently in a well-created database, so that employees who may need only generic demographic data don't accidentally have access to confidential student data. On the other hand, a principal of a school may very well want to look at an individual student's data and all its extensions—personal information, demographics, performance, discipline, extracurricular activities and so on—to get a true picture of where this student stands in school. A central data warehouse allows this kind of user-specific manipulation, usually based on a set of username login credentials. Sophisticated data warehouse and management systems may even allow web-based access from home for parents, to allow them to retrieve updates on their child's progress.

Good data warehouses also allow easy filtering of data. As mentioned previously, there are times when we want to look at a data overlay to consider, for example, students who are at risk of failing and who have also repeated a grade. From a data warehouse, a user would be able to create a data query to generate a streamlined report that presents just such data. If we wanted to find this same filtered set of data in the traditional way of asking around for cumulative folders, report cards, and so on, we could spend hours of time on the menial side of this endeavor before we actually got to the meat of what we wanted.

ESTABLISHING A DATA WAREHOUSE

Setting up a data warehouse can be a daunting task. You may find that numerous people across various areas have layers of data hiding out in binders and boxes. In some cases there are numerous files and databases with the exact same information but structured in completely different ways and saved in various formats. If you've got more than one piece of paper on which a person is asked to fill in the same data more than once, it's time to rethink your system.

The most effective way to begin the process of data warehousing is to meet with another school or district that has already begun this process. You'll get the inside scoop on vendor support, trouble spots with coordinating the data, user training needs, safety and security issues, and so on.

An effective data warehouse will help you:

- Streamline databases so that there is a core database containing all relevant information

- Verify the safety of the data in terms of duplicate backups and secure saves and updates

- Remove unnecessary duplication of data sets

- Remove unnecessary data from primary or core data sets

- Ensure that common terms are used throughout the school or district

Districts and schools must also come to an operational understanding and agreement on key data terms—for example, that they will use either the term *gender* or the term *sex*, and that those terms will not be interchangeable when it comes to reporting data. Further, an existing single field for phone number may need to be altered to allow a way to designate entries as "Primary Home Phone," "Primary Mobile Phone," and so on.

According to Keith Krueger, CEO of CoSN (Consortium for School Networking; www.cosn.org/3dm), "Districts using data-driven decision making estimate that they spend at least one year planning the system and developing community support for it." It's a good idea to coordinate the development of a data warehouse with the instructional and professional development side of this process. Use Worksheet 21—Data Warehouse Questions to help start the development process. Previous conversations surrounding the examination of existing data, identifying the various sources of data, and contemplating data overlays will have already set the ball rolling toward the establishment of a true data warehouse system.

One of the biggest lessons I've learned when working with schools and districts is that the most robust and meaty data warehouse system can be set up and function smoothly from a mechanical standpoint—but without ongoing training and a user-friendly interface, it doesn't provide much help in the overall instructional process. It cannot be stressed enough that no purchasing decisions should be made or contracts signed until the vendor has demonstrated the interface and its components to multiple audiences, including teachers, principals, central-office staff, secretaries, guidance counselors, and so on, to ensure that each of these users will be able to gain ready access to this system and understand its interface.

The data warehouse must also provide the customized functionality that makes sense for the end users. Guidance counselors will want to create data queries that look different from those created by individual classroom teachers. Principals will also want to be able to pull data in various ways that may be different from the needs of a special education coordinator, for example. A data warehouse must be robust enough that it can contain all the key data, keep it safe, ensure its integrity, and provide easy access to all its end users.

For additional considerations, visit the state of North Carolina's Frequently Asked Questions section for their statewide educational data warehouse (www.ncwise.org/ncwiseQuesFAQ.html). The questions and answers posed there can provide valuable insight into the day-to-day practical concerns and trouble spots that may arise. Worksheet 22—Key Questions to Ask Data Warehouse Committees and Vendors can help guide you in choosing an appropriate data warehouse system.

Regardless of where your school or district is in its quest to warehouse data centrally, it is important that end users be able to generate data reports to serve their needs. Scott McLeod's School Data Tutorials website (http://http://schooltechleadership.org/research/school-data-tutorials/) provides a wealth of easy-to-use tools designed to work with school data. These tools provide numerous methods and templates for educators who need to examine and report school data even from the most basic data sets, using easy spreadsheet tools. In addition, there are numerous resources and tutorials at the site, all dealing with school and district data.

WORKSHEET 19

Instructional Technology Checklist 1: What Do We Have?

- Do all teachers have their own teacher workstation?

  - Does it offer secure file storage available from anywhere?

  - Does it allow access to district mainframes for data use, curriculum resources, etc. if available?

  - Are teachers allowed to use this workstation from home if needed or desired?

- Does every classroom have multiple computers that are in good working order?

  - Can students print from these computers?

  - Can these computers connect to the Internet?

  - If these computers malfunction, is there a simple and quick system in place to get them repaired?

- Do our classrooms have ample technology-related components—projectors, presentation equipment, file storage, secure network access?

- Are there multiple avenues for students to use technology with each teacher—classroom-based, labs, mobile carts, mobile learning devices?

Instructional Technology Checklist 2: How Well Are We Using What We Have?

- Does *every* teacher meet our minimum expectations in regard to technology skills and proficiency?

    - For those who do, how do we continue to help them grow? How do we enable them to move forward without holding them back?

    - For those who do not, what concrete plans are in place to better educate and support them?

- How do our teachers demonstrate this proficiency on an ongoing basis?

- How well do our principals model effective technology use, relevant to their job duties?

- How well does leadership staff take advantage of technology-related resources to help them do their jobs?

- Do our teachers take part in ongoing, technology integration–related professional development that is beyond technical and managerial?

- Do our teachers make use of new and emerging technologies—Web 2.0, social sites, online collaborative tools, student production and publishing, video, audio, and so on?

- Do students, regardless of teacher placement, all have ample opportunities to take part in a highly engaged learning environment, supported by relevant and appropriate technology use?

- Do we take advantage of the technological savvy of our students by allowing them to take on support issues? Technology exploration, production, and maintenance? Are our teachers comfortable with letting students help them use the technology more effectively?

- Do we offer a balance between protecting our students from online risk, yet offering them ample opportunities to use technology to interact on a global scale? Does our filtering system support this balance?

Data Warehouse Questions

- Which combination of funds will be used to develop, build, and support this data warehouse?

- Who will be the key school/district liaisons (must include technical *and* instructional representation) in establishing vendor expectations? Who will attend preparatory meetings with potential vendors (must include technical *and* instructional representation)?

- What other schools/districts will we visit or consult with?

- What are our data reporting requirements at the local level? Department of Education level?

- What are the stages in our timeline toward rollout?

- Who will provide professional development for this warehouse? Technical support?

- How would this professional development fit into our plans for:

    - Data-driven decision making concepts and key instructional components

    - Data integrity, safety, security, and privacy issues

    - Data tools training—queries, reports, user interface

- Who will be our end users? What are their needs and requirements? What specific processes do our users undertake that pull from data?

- What pieces of this data system (if any) will be made available to parents? Community?

- What other management systems are in place? Can we build on what we have? Will our curriculum management system tie into a data warehouse system?

- Who will determine the level of access each user has to various data sets (e.g., when Mrs. Smith in School A logs into the data warehouse, what protocols are in place so that she does not have access to data from School B)?

Key Questions to Ask Data Warehouse Committees and Vendors

- Does the contract allow for ongoing and unlimited changes once the data warehouse begins to be available to end users? Staff may not have a clear picture for all data reporting templates until a specific situation arises. The data warehouse must be flexible enough to accommodate future needs, changes in data reporting requirements, and so on.

- What is the backup plan for this data? Loss or damage to data will be catastrophic. Describe the multiple backup process in detail, along with warranty and guarantee information.

- Data safety is of utmost concern professionally and legally. What safeguards are in place that secure this data from unauthorized personnel?

- Who will be the key school or district staff that interacts with the data warehouse provider for administrative policy issues, technical support, and so on?

- What are our sources of data in this school/district, and will each of these be able to be warehoused within this system?

- How will we migrate existing data sets into this data warehouse? What procedures are in place to make this a "clean" migration?

- Once data is in and secured, how will users manage various reports, data overlays, and other queries? How do we build these overlays? How are they saved so they don't have to be built from scratch each time the data is required?

- What *initial* training will be offered? What *additional* training will be offered? What end-user training and support will be available on an ongoing basis?

- In what schools/districts is this warehouse already in place, and how might we visit or contact existing users?

- Does this warehouse follow recognized data communication interoperability, such as that recommended by SIFA—the Schools Interoperability Framework Association (www.sifinfo.org)?

5

Engaging the Larger School Community

AS MEMBERS of the school and district become more knowledgeable about analyzing and using various measures of data, we must all be able to take a step backward and look at the big picture.

To what extent do we engage those *not* employed by the school system? Have we communicated key data, achievement, and improvement terms effectively to the larger school community? Have we considered new ways to use technology to involve hard-to-reach parents? Have we thought about the best ways to involve local businesses? Do students know how to make use of their own learning data? What does this entire learning environment look like from the outside?

A well-established, solid cycle of communications in a school community is critical in ensuring that schools get the help they need. Everyone involved in the school population should understand what is going on, what is being done to address any educational shortcomings, and how external assistance can best be directed.

Many of our parents and community partners have not been directly in touch with the classroom since they graduated. They may have children and grandchildren in school, but they rarely spend time inside classrooms. The homework today's students take home is different from the homework given when most parents were in school. The tools students use don't look the same, and the way students interact with each other and their teachers isn't the same either. These people may not have an accurate view of a current learning environment, because their descriptions of it may come only from their students or from what they read in the local newspaper about data and performance issues. How many times have we dealt with an angry parent, for example, only to find that the anger was a result of misinformation or miscommunication?

Districts working to create a more informed culture must examine how information reaches entities outside the building, and how well the district or school communicates its data accurately and constructively to its various audiences. Regularly sending out a mailing to parents that focuses on *good* news and explains just a few key issues the school or district will be working on in regard to data and school improvement is a must, of course. Many schools already do that now with the school newsletter. But, have schools considered that this traditional newsletter is also an opportunity to *collect* data that helps answer performance questions? Does your school communicate focused information to every business in the area? Distributing a bulletin explaining how the school is working to create the ultimate workforce can strike a chord with businesses in a way that a parent-oriented newsletter might not.

Reflect on the following avenues through which school data reaches the larger educational community. Consider how effectively and accurately data might be portrayed in each of these communication lines:

- School newsletters
- Parent/teacher conferences
- Parent Teacher Association or Organization meetings
- Classroom visits
- School board meetings
- Student to student
- Student to parent
- Parent to parent
- Newspapers and television reports
- Local business conversations
- Websites
- Social media feeds
- Social networking sites

If a school or district actively and regularly reexamines what data is communicated and how, it provides an opportunity for everyone to think more clearly about what is going on and offers targeted assistance where it is truly needed. Further, if the organization takes control of its communications and focuses its efforts in a more proactive way, it can align outside support with internal efforts.

Instead of waiting for test scores to be reported in the newspaper in the spring, why not report them now, along with efforts the school is making to address issues? How about having a few students speak at a local business roundtable about how they're employing technology to solve real-world problems, for example? In each of these cases, sharing some concrete performance data, along with a description of how the school is addressing this data, is a preemptive way to garner support and thwart uninformed criticism down the road.

The communications piece of the puzzle offers a way to incorporate data while soliciting encouragement from the community and engaging students and teachers with the world outside the classroom. A data-informed staff can work together to create highly customized newsletters, media briefings, presentations, social web blasts, and so on. A simple communications plan can incorporate numerous opportunities to promote student writing, publishing, communicating, collaborating, and research—all while solving real-world and community problems.

Talk with a local fast food chain to inquire about the possibility of printing tray liners to provide information about the school that informs parents of the *good* things happening. Include a few dates of upcoming school-related events. Invite the public to attend chorus concerts, plays, and so on. Include some key learning goals the school is trying to accomplish.

Many locally owned businesses now have websites and social networking pages. Whether a school creates a social network presence, or sticks with a traditional web page, linking this web effort to local businesses and other organizations can be a very efficient mechanism for sharing information. For example, ask a local business if they could promote a school/district initiative on their Facebook page. Instruct your students and parents to visit that page, and share comments. Some businesses like having parents join their social network page and point out what drove them there. For example, "I joined your page because I'm a proud parent at Patriot High School."

Use a template like the one provided in Worksheet 23—Data Communications Plan Template to map out some basic strategies for communicating data more concretely. Reflect on the audiences outside school with whom more direct information might be shared. Consider the audience, the types of data and information that seem *relevant* to that particular audience, the best avenue for communicating that information, and how this task might be taken on by students and teachers as an integrated part of the curriculum.

Communicating to parents is clearly a top priority. Traditional school newsletters serve a purpose, no doubt. But, a more targeted and purposeful communication effort can be an effective tool for solidifying support and understanding in the student, parent, and teacher relationship.

It is critical to keep in mind that effective communication isn't a one-way street. Getting data out to the public is important, but getting targeted data back *into* the school is just as vital. One easy method for soliciting parental feedback is to use a simple web-based survey. There are numerous online survey tools such as Survey Monkey (www.surveymonkey.com) or Google Forms (http://docs.google.com/templates) that are very easy to use. Perhaps the school or district wants to create a survey to get a feel for how learning continues once school is over. This survey might include questions about parental thoughts on home enrichment, computer access, and understanding of homework. Be clear in what you want back from parents, and communicate that effectively. The school has already spent time looking at internal performance data sets, so reflect back on those conversations to see if there were chunks of data missing that might be gained through a parent survey.

If you're going to take the time to create something more formal than a traditional Friday newsletter, be sure it communicates the appropriate message and solicits relevant feedback. Sample letters for eliciting parental and business feedback are provided on the following pages. Notice that each is tweaked to speak appropriately to the intended audience. Although both convey similar information and requests, they are different enough that the recipients are more likely to understand the information and be inclined to contribute back to the cycle of communication.

Parents,

Our school continues to work toward creating the most outstanding learning experiences for our students—your children. We have recently begun looking more closely at what our test scores tell us, paying closer attention to the environment in which we educate your child, and making plans to elevate what we expect out of this learning community as a whole.

As you are aware, each year we raise our performance goals. The past few years have been spent continuing to provide the excellent educational services we've always provided, enhanced with new strategies and higher expectations. There are also new testing measurements in place to help guide our efforts.

We've made numerous gains. Specifically, our math scores in middle school have shown continuous growth in the last three years. In the past, there was a noticeable difference between our high-school science scores and scores across the state. We've started to narrow that gap, and last year our science scores in 10th and 11th grade approached the state average. For a detailed listing of our school's "report card" please visit _____.

This letter is to inform you that we recognize how different the world is today from when we were all in school years ago. That means our expectations have changed—they are higher, tougher, and different. We will be working with you to make sure we can join forces and unite to make your child the best she or he can be. But, we need a renewed commitment from our parents. We want to reach out to you in new ways, and we hope you will join us in this undertaking.

If you have access to the Internet, please visit _____ to complete a short survey we've put together. Every household who completes the survey will be eligible for the chance to win a $25 gift card, donated by Chamber's Home Supply store. If you do not have Internet access, please call the school and we will be glad to mail you a paper copy. You can send this survey to school with your child, and your name will be entered into the drawing as well.

We will be hosting detailed updates at Hopewell Community Center next Monday, September 13th, at 5:30 p.m., and Wednesday, September 15th at 6:30 p.m. In addition, our board member from region 4 will be hosting a parent update session at Greenwood YMCA on September 20th at 6:30 p.m.

Finally, thank you. We have a lot to offer to your children, and we are proud to be doing so. We will be in touch again very soon.

Business Leaders,

Our district continues to work toward creating the most outstanding learning experiences for our students, *your current and future employees*. We have begun looking more closely at what our test scores tell us, paying closer attention to the environment in which we educate our students, and making plans to elevate what we expect out of this learning community as a whole. We have researched workforce trends, and it is our goal to provide a ready-to-work community.

As you are aware, each year we raise our performance goals. The past few years have been spent continuing to provide the excellent educational services we've always provided, enhanced with new strategies and higher expectations. There are also new testing measurements in place to help guide our efforts.

We've made numerous gains. Specifically, our math scores in middle school have shown improvement over where they were three years ago. This means our students are able to solve more complex mathematical, planning, and financial problems. In the past, there was a noticeable difference between our high-school science scores and higher scores across the state. We've started to narrow that gap, and last year our science scores in 10th and 11th grade approached the state average. Our students are now scientists, as opposed to learners of science. Our curriculum is more rigorous than ever before, and the payoff shows in how our schools perform. For a detailed listing of our school's "report card" please visit _____.

This letter is to inform you that we recognize how different the world is today from when we were all in school years ago. That means our expectations have changed—they are higher, tougher, and different. The workforce of today is drastically different than when most of us entered it years ago. We will be working with you to make sure we can join forces and unite to make the children of this community the best they can be. But, we need a renewed commitment from our businesses and community partners. We want to reach out to you in new ways, and we hope you will join us in this undertaking. It is critical that our schools reflect the 21st-century world around us. While we have expertise in learning theory and teaching strategies, we need *your insights* as far as what ideal graduates and employees look like and what they are able to do.

Please visit _____ to complete a short survey we've put together. Every business that enters will be featured in the local newspaper as a proud supporter of our high school, and will be eligible to win a free, full-page ad in our school yearbook. If you prefer, you can obtain a printed copy of the survey by calling the school. You can mail this survey to the address included, and your business will be entered into the drawing as well.

Finally, thank you. Our student population is your workforce and market. We are proud to work in conjunction with you, and your feedback will be crucial in helping us chart our course.

New Methods for Parental Interactions

Educating our parents and businesses about new expectations for learning and new school environments is a solid step toward creating a well-informed school community. However, we must take a calculated approach to this piece of the improvement plan. We must make deliberate attempts to involve parents and community in *unique* ways.

We can provide novel ways to get parents involved, obtain parental feedback, and better inform our parents. Some schools now provide parents a chance to view school videos and sample lessons online through webinars or social media sites. Some even provide short training and informational sessions online, opening up another avenue in which to lift the entire learning community's level of expertise and understanding of a 21st-century, data-informed entity.

Has your school considered allowing students to provide some free parent training in a computer lab after school hours? If a technology class partnered with a language class, perhaps a session could intertwine writing, publishing, and technology skills in a project that enlightens our parental community about 21st-century classrooms. How about workshops for parents on how they can maximize free online tools for personal productivity? Some schools have found specific workshops like "How to Use an Online Calendar to Manage a Busy Household" hugely popular. Perhaps these workshops could even be put online, in the form of a podcast or webinar, so parents could take part at their leisure. In each workshop or online presentation, the school has an opportunity to communicate a "commercial" about its data, current school efforts or needs, and so on. Get parents into the habit of realizing that the school their child attends isn't an isolated building in which learning happens only inside four-walled classrooms, but rather a hub of learning, communication, and information in which everyone has an active, important role. A sample agenda for a "kickoff" parent meeting follows, which introduces parents to the thought of working together in new ways.

Rethinking how we communicate with parents, businesses, and the rest of the educational community is a crucial part of a data-enriched culture. Student work creates data, teacher planning creates data, formative and summative assessments create data, and humans interacting and communicating with each other creates data. Getting a handle on which data to communicate in which way and to whom helps the education machine operate more efficiently and effectively. This can also be one method for removing hurdles and addressing misinformation outside the school. Having a welcomed and well-informed public makes everyone's jobs easier and, in the long run, helps us provide a more streamlined service to our entire education community.

Agenda

PARENTAL COLLABORATION MEETING ONE

5:30 p.m.   Welcome and snacks provided by athletic department

5:40 p.m.   School-specific performance issues
> *Where we stand on school performance goals, what this means for our district/school*

6:00 p.m.   21st-century homework overview
> *Homework expectations, the different look and feel, project-based learning, benefits, students explain new homework strategies*

6:20 p.m.   Computer lab activities
> *Wikipedia for parents (students provide one-on-one assistance to parents)*

6:55 p.m.   Parental online survey
> *Priorities for students*
> *Expectations for parent/teacher collaborations*
> *Suggestions for community/school collaborations*

7:05 p.m.   Overview of our new "Workday Webinars" & schedule
> *Free 20-minute online parental updates developed, produced, and delivered by students*

7:15 p.m.   Drawing for door prize
> *One free hour of home tech support from Computer Club*

OCTOBER WEBINAR DATES

10:00 a.m.   October 1
> 21st-Century Learning provided by seventh grade Science

11:00 a.m.   October 12
> Digital Photography in Action provided by sixth grade History

12:00 p.m.   October 22
> Free online tools for busy parents provided by eighth grade Language Arts

23

Data Communications Plan Template

COMMUNITY RECIPIENT	MEDIA/METHOD	MESSAGE/DATA	CREATOR
Example: Ralph's Lawnmower Repair	Website	"Did you know Watkins High School has cut its dropout rate for the 3rd year in a row?"	Arts & Media class
Example: CinemaPlex II	Ad preceding movie preview	"Top 5 reasons you should see LaGrange Elementary"	Computer Club
Example: Business Roundtable	In-Person presentation	"Workforce skills we address in 7th grade—how and why"	Middle grades Civics class
Example: KLOE radio station	On-air ads promoting the school's social network page	Ongoing instructional events that warrant parent and community involvement	School library media center

6

Reflecting on the Progress

DATA-DRIVEN decision making isn't an initiative. It isn't something else we pile on top of the existing things we do. It's a way of thinking and a mode of operation. It's a state of mind that might not necessarily come naturally to us. Increased demands for accountability have put new pressure on students and teachers. We live in a fast-paced world, and we may sometimes get into the habit of making decisions without adequate reflection time. Working together to envision a big picture and acting as a unified 3D team to work toward that vision relieves some of that pressure. To move our entire educational machine forward in a healthy way, we must take concrete steps to analyze our educational community and its various layers. We must be able to take a hard look at barriers that prevent us from advancing. Finally, we must all be held responsible, no matter what our role, for ensuring that our district and schools operate in the most efficient, well-informed manner possible.

At this point, schools and districts have identified key student performance data trends and issues, examined existing resources, and worked on communicating needs and expectations more efficiently. We now need to think "big picture" once again to ensure that we aren't overwhelming ourselves and that our organization is working efficiently as a whole. One method for this is continuously reflecting on which initiatives fit into the overall vision or mission of the school and ensuring that these efforts intertwine as efficiently as possible. School administrators tend to grab onto initiatives because they are stuck in a corner, feeling desperate to make changes and improve student outcomes. However, simply piling one program on top of another sometimes has detrimental effects in that it can actually lower teacher efficiency and raise burnout and exhaustion levels.

The 3D team can lead ongoing reflection conversations to get some informal data about how teachers feel about the coordination of initiatives across the building(s). It is important, of course, to frame this in a positive light, because the goal of this activity is to collect relevant data and use that data to refine or streamline efforts.

Here is a way to start the schoolwide coordination and alignment reflection conversation:

1. Brainstorm as a group, a list of initiatives, activities, or programs the school takes part in, regardless of whether teachers individually chose that program or it was prescribed to the school.

2. Consider the following questions:

    a. Where is there overlap among these programs?

    b. Is this a positive overlap, in that the programs complement each other, or are they repetitive without being complementary?

    c. If they are repetitive without being complementary, how might they be adjusted to better support the goals of each?

    d. If this can't be done, should one of the programs be dropped? Who will be affected by dropping this program? What will be gained by dropping this program? What effect would the elimination have on student achievement?

3. Are there pieces of this overall picture that aren't available? For example, could an initiative or program be escalated to include more teachers or more students?

4. What data do we have that suggests that these programs, either individually or as a combined group, supports student achievement in some way? Be certain to look beyond test scores.

Here is a way to start the district-level coordination and alignment reflection conversation:

1. As a cabinet or central-office leadership staff, brainstorm a list of key initiatives that are provided to schools and teachers, and which department prescribed these initiatives to the school.

2. Consider the following questions:

    a. How informed is one department about solutions and programs being provided by other departments?

    b. Do we know what these programs are about?

    c. Where do our programs overlap with others? Is this a positive overlap, in that the programs complement each other, or are they repetitive without being complementary?

    d. If they are repetitive without being complementary, how might they be adjusted to better support the goals of each? How might they be better aligned or coordinated?

    e. How is each program funded? Could these funds complement each other?

3. How is professional development provided to support these programs? Could this professional development be coordinated? Delivered at the same time in the same way?

4. What data do we have that suggests that these programs, either individually or as a combined group, actually support student achievement in some way? Be certain to look beyond test scores.

5. Are these programs being rolled out in a way that doesn't demand unnecessary time from teachers?

Coordination and alignment of efforts is absolutely crucial for schools. Getting data from program coordinators and participants that paints a picture of program efficiency and alignment of initiatives helps to make the organization a better-oiled machine. Further, ensuring that we collect data that supports the time, effort, and money spent on these programs is a must. The big picture of data-driven decision making requires each of the key players to reflect on what they bring to the table, what they take away, what impact their programs provide right now, and the legacy these programs leave behind. It is important that these kinds of brainstorming sessions be held annually at the very least.

Keeping the Data-Informed Culture Alive and Well

It cannot be stressed enough that data-driven decision making isn't a workshop. It doesn't end when the school year ends, or when test scores come back from the state department. It's a mindset that leaders must exemplify and model to make the most informed decision possible.

Leading this culture takes a first step, which is to begin the conversation and ask some critical questions. It takes commitment from all levels of the education community. It requires that we ask tough questions and commit to following up on those questions. It demands that we make decisions that are truly informed by some set of data, and that we check up on those decisions in an ongoing way to ensure that we are progressing as planned. It requires that we communicate our data and our plans to the bigger audience, and expect that they communicate back to us in a cyclical way. It also pushes us to put our heads together and join forces to make our educational community efficient, informed, and focused.

Glossary

3D team. A data-driven decision (3D) team who rallies together to help move forward the concept and culture of data-driven and data-informed decision making.

data-driven decision making. The ongoing cycle of making choices based on multiple sources of data and frequent, thoughtful conversations—*the concept of data-driven decision making is a mindset and a culture, not an initiative.*

disaggregate. To break down data from a larger, aggregated format such as a schoolwide performance list, to smaller subsets of data in order to gain a more detailed view.

formative assessment. Ongoing, usually short-term assessments designed to estimate progress in the midst of a unit to help predict and inform success thus far.

leader. Anyone, regardless of title or official function, who steps to the front to champion a cause, change, or way of thinking.

professional learning community. A collaborative culture in which the entire educational team takes part in frequent, productive, professional conversations and activities aimed at improving school culture and performance or personal growth.

root cause. The most basic reason for a problem or issue. In terms of educational data, it means getting beyond a surface level symptom, and exploring down as far as one can go in order to get to something concretely addressable.

standardized test. A test that is developed and administered to measure student achievement in a manner that provides a uniform measurement across geographic boundaries, environments, and so on.

Stanford 10. Stanford Achievement Test series.

summative assessment. The assessment of student progress in a more systemic and formal way, generally used to summarize student learning over time, typically given at the end of a unit or academic year.

webinar. A web-based "how to" training session delivered via the Internet to your computer.

Wikipedia. A free, online, user-built "living" encyclopedia.

Internet Resources

DATA COLLECTION/MANAGEMENT TOOLS

CoSN—Consortium for School Networking Data Resources
www.cosn.org/3dm

Data Wikispace
(typical definitions, online support materials)
http://leadingdata.wikispaces.com

Education for the Future
http://eff.csuchico.edu

School Data Tutorials
(spreadsheet templates for data collection, disaggregation, and discussion)
http://schooltechleadership.org/teaching/school-data-tutorials

Scott McLeod's data-driven decision making resources
http://scottmcleod.net/resources/dddm/

US Department of Education Resource Portal
www.eddataexpress.ed.gov

SURVEY TOOLS

Google Forms
http://docs.google.com/templates

ProfilerPro—Collaborative Profiler Survey Tool
http://profilerpro.com

Survey Monkey
http://surveymonkey.com

BRAINSTORMING TOOLS

Inspiration
www.inspiration.com

Gliffy
www.gliffy.com

Bubbl.us
http://bubbl.us

DATA WAREHOUSING RESOURCES

Schools Interoperability Framework Association
www.sifinfo.org

Data Warehouse Frequently Asked Questions and Issues to Consider
www.ncwise.org/ncwiseQuesFAQ.html

DIGITAL CALENDARS FOR COLLABORATION

Google Calendar
http://calendar.google.com

Yahoo Calendar
http://calendar.yahoo.com

National Educational Technology Standards for Teachers and Administrators

NETS for Teachers (NETS•T)

All classroom teachers should be prepared to meet the following standards and performance indicators.

1. **Facilitate and Inspire Student Learning and Creativity**

   Teachers use their knowledge of subject matter, teaching and learning, and technology to facilitate experiences that advance student learning, creativity, and innovation in both face-to-face and virtual environments. Teachers:

   a. promote, support, and model creative and innovative thinking and inventiveness

   b. engage students in exploring real-world issues and solving authentic problems using digital tools and resources

   c. promote student reflection using collaborative tools to reveal and clarify students' conceptual understanding and thinking, planning, and creative processes

   d. model collaborative knowledge construction by engaging in learning with students, colleagues, and others in face-to-face and virtual environments

2. **Design and Develop Digital-Age Learning Experiences and Assessments**

   Teachers design, develop, and evaluate authentic learning experiences and assessments incorporating contemporary tools and resources to maximize content learning in context and to develop the knowledge, skills, and attitudes identified in the NETS•S. Teachers:

   a. design or adapt relevant learning experiences that incorporate digital tools and resources to promote student learning and creativity

   b. develop technology-enriched learning environments that enable all students to pursue their individual curiosities and become active participants in setting their own educational goals, managing their own learning, and assessing their own progress

    c.   customize and personalize learning activities to address students' diverse learning styles, working strategies, and abilities using digital tools and resources

    d.   provide students with multiple and varied formative and summative assessments aligned with content and technology standards and use resulting data to inform learning and teaching

3.   **Model Digital-Age Work and Learning**

Teachers exhibit knowledge, skills, and work processes representative of an innovative professional in a global and digital society. Teachers:

    a.   demonstrate fluency in technology systems and the transfer of current knowledge to new technologies and situations

    b.   collaborate with students, peers, parents, and community members using digital tools and resources to support student success and innovation

    c.   communicate relevant information and ideas effectively to students, parents, and peers using a variety of digital-age media and formats

    d.   model and facilitate effective use of current and emerging digital tools to locate, analyze, evaluate, and use information resources to support research and learning

4.   **Promote and Model Digital Citizenship and Responsibility**

Teachers understand local and global societal issues and responsibilities in an evolving digital culture and exhibit legal and ethical behavior in their professional practices. Teachers:

    a.   advocate, model, and teach safe, legal, and ethical use of digital information and technology, including respect for copyright, intellectual property, and the appropriate documentation of sources

    b.   address the diverse needs of all learners by using learner-centered strategies and providing equitable access to appropriate digital tools and resources

    c.   promote and model digital etiquette and responsible social interactions related to the use of technology and information

    d.   develop and model cultural understanding and global awareness by engaging with colleagues and students of other cultures using digital-age communication and collaboration tools

5. **Engage in Professional Growth and Leadership**

    Teachers continuously improve their professional practice, model lifelong learning, and exhibit leadership in their school and professional community by promoting and demonstrating the effective use of digital tools and resources. Teachers:

    a. participate in local and global learning communities to explore creative applications of technology to improve student learning

    b. exhibit leadership by demonstrating a vision of technology infusion, participating in shared decision making and community building, and developing the leadership and technology skills of others

    c. evaluate and reflect on current research and professional practice on a regular basis to make effective use of existing and emerging digital tools and resources in support of student learning

    d. contribute to the effectiveness, vitality, and self-renewal of the teaching profession and of their school and community

NETS for Administrators (NETS•A)

All school administrators should be prepared to meet the following standards and performance indicators.

1. **Visionary Leadership**

    Educational Administrators inspire and lead development and implementation of a shared vision for comprehensive integration of technology to promote excellence and support transformation throughout the organization. Educational Administrators:

    a. inspire and facilitate among all stakeholders a shared vision of purposeful change that maximizes use of digital-age resources to meet and exceed learning goals, support effective instructional practice, and maximize performance of district and school leaders

    b. engage in an ongoing process to develop, implement, and communicate technology-infused strategic plans aligned with a shared vision

    c. advocate on local, state, and national levels for policies, programs, and funding to support implementation of a technology-infused vision and strategic plan

2. **Digital-Age Learning Culture**

    Educational Administrators create, promote, and sustain a dynamic, digital-age learning culture that provides a rigorous, relevant, and engaging education for all students. Educational Administrators:

    a. ensure instructional innovation focused on continuous improvement of digital-age learning

    b. model and promote the frequent and effective use of technology for learning

    c. provide learner-centered environments equipped with technology and learning resources to meet the individual, diverse needs of all learners

    d. ensure effective practice in the study of technology and its infusion across the curriculum

    e. promote and participate in local, national, and global learning communities that stimulate innovation, creativity, and digital-age collaboration

3. **Excellence in Professional Practice**

    Educational Administrators promote an environment of professional learning and innovation that empowers educators to enhance student learning through the infusion of contemporary technologies and digital resources. Educational Administrators:

    a. allocate time, resources, and access to ensure ongoing professional growth in technology fluency and integration

    b. facilitate and participate in learning communities that stimulate, nurture, and support administrators, faculty, and staff in the study and use of technology

    c. promote and model effective communication and collaboration among stakeholders using digital-age tools

    d. stay abreast of educational research and emerging trends regarding effective use of technology and encourage evaluation of new technologies for their potential to improve student learning

4. **Systemic Improvement**

    Educational Administrators provide digital-age leadership and management to continuously improve the organization through the effective use of information and technology resources. Educational Administrators:

    a. lead purposeful change to maximize the achievement of learning goals through the appropriate use of technology and media-rich resources

    b. collaborate to establish metrics, collect and analyze data, interpret results, and share findings to improve staff performance and student learning

    c. recruit and retain highly competent personnel who use technology creatively and proficiently to advance academic and operational goals

    d. establish and leverage strategic partnerships to support systemic improvement

    e. establish and maintain a robust infrastructure for technology including integrated, interoperable technology systems to support management, operations, teaching, and learning

5. **Digital Citizenship**

Educational Administrators model and facilitate understanding of social, ethical, and legal issues and responsibilities related to an evolving digital culture. Educational Administrators:

    a. ensure equitable access to appropriate digital tools and resources to meet the needs of all learners

    b. promote, model, and establish policies for safe, legal, and ethical use of digital information and technology

    c. promote and model responsible social interactions related to the use of technology and information

    d. model and facilitate the development of a shared cultural understanding and involvement in global issues through the use of contemporary communication and collaboration tools